CREATING COMMON GROUND CONNECTIONS

Through an empathetic and positive approach to interpersonal communication, this book guides readers to build on the skills they already possess to communicate—and connect—with others.

Author David W. Bennett, Ph.D. approaches communication with the belief that it is at the heart of any human division. This book helps readers find a way to communicate that will help build understanding regardless of each party's perspective. Written in an approachable and conversational style, the book includes tips, examples, and concept reviews to easily illustrate communication principles readers can take with them beyond their courses or training sessions.

An ideal supplement to courses focusing on skills in interpersonal, professional, or business communication, this book can also be used as a communication primer for students or professionals in any field.

David W. Bennett, Ph.D. teaches Interpersonal Communication and Introduction to Public Speaking at Ivy Tech Community College, USA. He is the owner of Common Ground Communication Training and Consulting, www.common-ground-communication.org.

CREATING COMMON GROUND CONNECTIONS

Healing Divisiveness

David W. Bennett

Routledge
Taylor & Francis Group

NEW YORK AND LONDON

Designed cover image: LeoPatrizi/Getty Images

First published 2023
by Routledge
605 Third Avenue, New York, NY 10158

and by Routledge
4 Park Square, Milton Park, Abingdon, Oxon, OX14 4RN

Routledge is an imprint of the Taylor & Francis Group, an informa business

ISBN: 978-1-032-41258-0 (hbk)
ISBN: 978-1-032-41257-3 (pbk)
ISBN: 978-1-003-35704-9 (ebk)

DOI: 10.4324/9781003357049

Typeset in Bembo
by Apex CoVantage, LLC

CONTENTS

PREFACE

You can make a difference

It's apparent over the last few years that people perceive the world to be deeply divided. People seem to be increasingly entrenched in their beliefs and rarely willing to entertain other ways of thinking.

How do we re-unite this world? Change starts with each person and how they communicate one-on-one with one another. That change then spreads outward through our communities, nations, and ultimately our world. It catches on because it works and taps into the basic desire for all people to communicate effectively with one another.

Each person can start this process by utilizing their natural common ground and connection skills. When you establish common ground with others, you seek to find things you have in common with them. It's hard to communicate with someone with whom you have nothing in common.

If you discover a trait or characteristic that you have in common with another person, then you can go further with that characteristic to create a connection. Connection goes deeper and more personal between both people. When you connect with someone, you and the other person are literally thinking in the same ways. Each person communicates with understanding. They "click."

In other words, one of the goals of this book is to increase people's awareness of skills they already possess, and then learn to use them more frequently and deliberately than they might do now. Those skills may be slightly different for each person based on with whom they interact and the situations in which they find themselves. That's the ultimate goal of this approach: to help people deliberately yet flexibly use these natural skills in all their conversations. Readers use their other communication skills which currently work for them to help create common ground connections in every conversation.

Chapter sections

To support your efforts in enhancing your communication ability are the following sections in each chapter:

1. **Current state of the world:** At the beginning of each chapter is a description of the divisiveness in the United States and the world today pertaining to the subject of each chapter. This sets the context for applying the concepts covered in the rest of the chapter.
2. **Chapter on "personal change":** A chapter is dedicated to helping the reader track their attempts at implementing common ground, connections, and common ground connections in their personal communication.

1

CREATING COMMON GROUND CONNECTIONS

Preview of book

Common ground connections, healing divisiveness

This book seeks to detail a new approach to communicating with the people of the world. "Common ground connections" is specially geared toward communicating with people with whom you disagree but can also make your existing relationships closer.

DOI:10.4324/9781003357049-1

The following chapters provide you with the most important information from each communication area set within the context of what can often be a divided world. Specifically, there are nine chapters:

Table of contents

Chapter abstracts

Chapter 1: creating common ground connections

This chapter introduces a new approach to communicating with others called common ground connections. The approach combines the establishment of common ground with the creation of mutual connections with others. When these natural skills are combined, you achieve the communication advantages of common ground and connection separately, and the advantages of combining both skill sets.

The United States and the world appear to be increasingly divisive and polarized. Ninety-three percent of people in the United States and 65% of people in the world believe it's important to reduce this divisiveness and realize more common ground. Most are still seeking progressive change through reasoned, peaceful discourse in ways that are available to them.

Common ground connections don't have to happen with just a significant other or close friend with whom we might share our most personal feelings. Connections can happen with a grocery store clerk, your hair stylist, or a complete stranger. These are connections too.

Chapter 2: conflict management

An inevitable part of all communication is conflict even with people we know well. Common ground connections can be difficult because two people regardless of their relationship can disagree with or misunderstand one another. You may have had the experience of getting into a major argument with even a close friend. It may be that you just can't understand how they're viewing a particular issue.

In order to create common ground connections in these conflict situations, we need to understand how each of us thinks about conflict, how others perceive conflict with us, and how each of us generally deals with conflict. This chapter provides flexible strategies for using the common ground connections approach to deal with your unique conflict situations.

Chapter 3: the unconscious communicator

Our brains have an almost unlimited capacity to process information. We don't always tap into that resource when we're communicating, however. You have to learn to "actively" think about the conversation in which you're engaged. It requires all parties to use their mind and observations to be flexible and adaptable in using common ground connection skills and their existing communication skills.

The vast majority of our communication is unconscious or automatic. We often don't think much about it. Sometimes that works for us, sometimes not. If you want to establish common ground connections, you have to bring more of your communication to conscious awareness.

Chapter 4: empathy

A survey of more than 19,400 people in 27 countries found that a majority of people in 25 of 27 countries think their society is divided (Duffy & Gottfried, 2018). Eighty-four percent of Americans feel the United States is divided along a number of lines. Over 90% of the people in Serbia, Argentina, Chile, and Peru feel their country is divided.

What's more concerning is that one action that might start to work on this divisiveness—empathy—is declining in the world. People seem to be increasingly anxious, unhappy, angry, and have decreased in their ability or willingness to use empathy (Decline in Human Empathy, 2019).

This chapter defines the basics of empathy, explains tools that can be used to demonstrate empathy, describes unique aspects of empathy, talks about how to avoid becoming overwhelmed when showing empathy, and the link between empathy and common ground connections.

Chapter 5: targeted speaking and nonverbal pinpointing

Targeted speaking

This chapter focuses on the details of spoken communication, the differences between our verbal and nonverbal communication, and a technique to best create common ground connections called targeted speaking. When you target your speaking, you adjust your language throughout each conversation to make sure the other person can understand what you're sharing. You use this skill all the time in a typical conversation. Labeling it "targeted" speaking is merely calling your attention to the fact that it's a good idea, and that you might want to try to use it more often.

Nonverbal pinpointing

In order to be successful in getting the information needed to create common ground connections, you need to tune into what can be a largely **untapped** source of information—nonverbal communication. Untapped because you tend to focus on what people say, not what they do. And yet most of the meaning in a conversation is carried in the nonverbal channel.

This section of the chapter introduces a new concept in understanding the nonverbal communication of others called nonverbal pinpointing. Nonverbal pinpointing is learning to identify specific nonverbal behaviors that will give you the best chance of understanding the other person in the present conversation. You consciously choose which nonverbal information to process and what to ignore.

Chapter 6: listen energetically

The most important communication factor in achieving a common ground connection with another person is your willingness to really listen to them. We spend more time listening to others than we do in any other communication activity.

A new emphasis—"energetic" listening—is explained as a way to enhance your existing listening skills. Energetic listening is listening with your whole self and with a high level of concentration and focus. More than anything it's a state of mind in which you mentally lock onto another person. Everyone listens. Not everyone listens energetically.

Chapter 7: sharing perceptions

When we communicate we seek to create a similar reality with the other person by "sharing" our perceptions. These shared perceptions are really the first step in communication, and the first step in building a common ground connection. Simply, we don't always see what someone else sees. Sometimes, however, we forget this when we're in an actual conversation.

What might be an obvious interpretation of an event to you might not be so obvious to another person. This chapter helps you get a handle on what can be a difficult part of communication—perception, and the importance of sharing perceptions in creating common ground connections.

Chapter 8: creating personal change

This chapter provides readers with realistic and usable guidelines for adopting the common ground connections approach to enhance their personal communication.

1. **Personal assessment:** This section provides a chart assessing the reader's current communication skill set. What are their current strengths? What do they believe they need to work on?

2. **Past common ground connection conversations:** Readers are asked to describe a conversation in the past in which they felt like they created common ground, connections, and common ground connections with others. As readers begin using common ground connections, they are asked to describe their experiences in each conversation including the benefits realized. Included in that tracking are comments about how the people with whom they had conversations may have reacted to their different conversational approach.

3. **Communication goals:** This section asks readers to write out specific goal statements to help them in transitioning to a common ground connection approach.

4. **Conflict situations:** Readers are asked to document the conversations in the past in which they've conflicted with someone. They're given guidance as to how to assess these situations. Then they're guided as to how they might use the common ground connections approach to improve these situations.

5. **Personality factors:** This section explains the impact of personality on changing personal communication: 1) selfishness, 2) obliviousness, 3) ego, and 4) desire to control.

6. **Personal change guidelines:** 1) use skills that fit your personality, 2) adapt the skills to your various relationships, 3) be patient with yourself, and 4) determine your motivation.

Chapter 9: healing a broken world

This chapter lays out the possibilities of common ground connections spreading from individuals and their immediate circle of friends and family to the rest of the world. It asks the question: "How might that happen?" and what can each of us do to share commonalities with others to facilitate that spread? We just need to get behind the idea that we're more alike than different and keep working to try to understand one another.

★★★

Chapter 1: creating common ground connections

Communication is at the heart of the division in the world just as it is at the heart of any human division. When we stop communicating with one another, the resolution of conflicts and disagreement becomes impossible. If we're going to continue to move forward, we need to find a way for people to communicate that will help them understand one another regardless of their perspective. That includes a willingness to not only try to understand other perspectives but also the willingness to consider that our own opinions might need to change.

The realities of communication

If we believe that different communication is the answer to the divisions in the world, we must first convince people that they need to change how they communicate now. This can be tough because people usually think they communicate pretty well. Most people would estimate their communication skills at 80–90% effectiveness. And why wouldn't people judge themselves so positively? They've been communicating since they were born. They've developed a way of communicating that they believe works for them.

Think of your own communication. You've generally learned what works, and what doesn't. You've created a set of communication skills that make up "your style" that works for you most of the time.

The problem with this is that sometimes your current communication skills don't work. When you have misunderstandings with others, you're confused by what someone says, or have a knock-down, drag-out argument with a significant other, your skills aren't working. Unfortunately, we often forget those times when communication doesn't go so well. No one wants to remember those few times when communication is just plain bad.

And to make matters worse, when our conversations don't go well, we often fail to take responsibility for it. We blame the other person for the problem or write it off as a one-time event. This mindset doesn't help us to resolve the problem.

So in the face of the challenges you face in communicating with others, are there skills you can focus on that will give you the best chance of "success," however, two people define that? Are there any existing skills all of us possess and use on a regular basis to try to communicate with each other at a deep level? It would be good if we already possessed those skills. That would only require us to use existing skills more deliberately, more often, or in different ways.

Preview of chapter

How do we re-unite this world? Change starts with each person and how they communicate one-on-one with one another. That change then spreads outward through our communities, nations, and ultimately our world. It catches on because it works and taps into the basis of all human interaction—communication with one another.

Each person can start this process by utilizing their natural common ground and connection skills. When you establish common ground with others, you seek to find things you have in common with them. It's hard to communicate with someone with whom you have nothing in common. Sometimes you go deeper than common ground and create a "connection" with someone. Connecting with others means the two people are literally thinking in the same ways. Each person thoroughly understands the other.

Combining common ground and connecting into common ground connections just makes sense. The skills of common ground connection are already a natural part of everyone's communication skills. Unfortunately, they often don't use them deliberately and in all their conversations. They miss opportunities to get close to and understand others through their communication.

You'll have an idea of the benefits of adopting this new approach because you've realized them already. You can probably remember conversations in the past in which you really felt close to someone. You may have just had a good "feeling" that you were sharing something special with that person.

In other words, one of the goals of this book is to increase people's awareness of skills they already possess, and then learn to use them more frequently and deliberately than they might do now. Those skills may be slightly different for each person based on with whom they interact and in different situations. The ultimate goal of this approach is to help people deliberately yet flexibly use these natural skills in all their conversations.

Particularly with people with whom you disagree, finding common ground connections will help you. You may have tried various things to fix the communication problems in some of your troubled relationships without success. The common ground connection approach may provide you with the answers for which you've been looking.

Chapter contents:

1. Common ground and connecting
2. Establishing common ground
3. Creating "connections"
4. Combining common ground and connections
5. Where do you start?
6. Success factors: personal perspectives and your mind
7. Overall benefits of creating common ground connections
8. It's not always as easy as it seems
9. Best situations to use common ground connections
10. When common ground connections don't work
11. Can one person change the world?

1. Common ground and connecting

"It just happens"

We often don't consciously establish common ground or seek to "connect" with others. Instead, it sometimes just "happens." You're having a conversation and one or both of you realize—"I didn't realize we had so much in common. We're really connected in so many ways."

The skills of common ground and connection are really a phenomenon in our communication. We don't seem to use them deliberately, but when we do we realize how powerful these skills are. Even when we experience how good it feels to establish common ground and create connections, we often forget to use them in our next conversation. If we could just tap into these skills and use them more deliberately and in every conversation, we could enhance our current communication in significant ways.

2. Establishing common ground

Finding common ground with others simply means we find things we have in common with them. We share interests, ideas, and even personal information about ourselves. We find commonalities not just differences. When we talk with people with whom we disagree, finding common ground will help us start a more productive dialogue with those people.

Everyone has established common ground with others. When you meet someone for the first time, what do you usually do? You usually ask some basic questions like what do they like to do in their spare time, what do they do for a living, and where do they live. When you get the answers to these and other basic "demographic" questions in other words you begin to understand that person. It simply makes it easier to communicate with someone with whom you have some things in common. If, for example, you're both in the accounting field, you know that both of you share an interest in that profession. Your shared interest in accounting is the start of establishing some basic common ground. You do this because it's difficult to communicate with another person if you don't share anything in common. For one thing, you may not have anything to talk about.

Establishing common ground doesn't just happen with people you're meeting for the first time either. You also continue to establish common ground with people you know well like family, friends, and spouses. For example, how many times have you been talking to a friend and found out something completely new about them? It could be a revelation that your friend Sarah was once the lead singer in a band. Since you have an interest in music and play the guitar, this may open up new avenues for your friendship with her. This is common ground too that helps people build more meaningful relationships over time.

Particularly with people with whom you disagree, finding areas on which you agree is a great start to understanding one another. You've probably had the experience of finding more areas of agreement than disagreement when you really work to resolve a disagreement. Finding commonalities in this way is a challenge but it can be done.

3. Creating "connections"

Sometimes, we go deeper than common ground and create a "connection" with someone. When you move from establishing common ground to connecting with another person, you're really seeking a more personal common ground. Connecting with others means the two people are literally thinking in the same way. It might be that you're talking to a person and suddenly get a real sensation that both of you have established a closeness, a high level of agreement, and even a shared consciousness. You could literally finish each other's sentences. A conversation that is free from confusion or judgment is created. The two people are mentally communicating as one. You might have thought: We're really in sync.

Connection doesn't always have to be some super close connection either. You can connect with anyone including the grocery store checkout person, a salesperson in a department store, or someone standing in line at your favorite fast food restaurant. The connection you establish with that "stranger" is still a connection because you're communicating for that brief moment in a way that both people can understand and feel good about.

For example, think of a time when you were going through a relationship breakup with your boyfriend. You were having trouble coping with the situation for a number of reasons primarily because the relationship had lasted so long. A caring friend really listened to you and tried to understand without telling you what to do. You "sensed" sincere empathy and compassion from the other person. It felt good to communicate with someone who cared. You felt a real connection with your friend. In the midst of your struggles, you "felt good" about the communication you shared.

Many authors have tried to specifically describe the experience of connecting. Maybe you've felt or experienced some of these characteristics yourself. Hobson (2018) thinks that there are two ways to describe connection: (1) the conversation just flows and (2) you click with someone. Hobcroft (2017) understands connecting as a sense of being open and available to another person, just as they are open and available to us. According to Ng (2017), connection includes at least the following four factors:

1. Empathy and compassion for another person
2. Taking the time to listen
3. Feeling listened to and understood
4. Kindness toward one another

Humans need to feel connected. Research has consistently shown that basic human connections are important to our well-being. Seppala (2012) points to a range of studies supporting the idea that social connection contributes to our health, well-being, and longevity.

So while we have some idea of how to connect with others, there is no list of mental and physical characteristics that we can point to and say: "That's connection." Connection can mean different things to different people. It can vary from conversation to conversation. What's clear is that if both people in a conversation are really open, trusting, and make an effort, deep connections can happen.

Particularly with people with whom you have an ongoing relationship you'll learn through your conversations the most likely ways to really connect with them.

You can't try to apply the same set of skills in all your conversations with that person but you do have a communication history with them on which you can draw.

4. Combining common ground and connections

When you combine the establishment of common ground with the creation of connections, you have the common ground connections approach. You'll have to actively think about this new way of communicating in every conversation with every person and then adjust accordingly. You'll soon begin to "sense" when you're being successful. Your existing communication skills will help you with this.

There's often a fine line between establishing common ground and seeking connections. They're really intertwined in real time in a conversation. They're slightly different concepts, but they also naturally work together. For example, you may be talking with a friend about her recent business trip to Houston. You ask about her experience flying from Milwaukee to Houston. She relates that the airline lost her bags. You ask her how she dealt with the situation. How did she feel—angry, frustrated, hopeless? You're still focused on her experience, but within that focus you may also share similar experiences you've had on your own business trips. This is how you create a connection that over time builds a more personal relationship.

5. Where do you start?

The first step in developing common ground connections is to be aware of the existing opportunities you have to use this approach in your daily conversations. Transitioning to this approach means you'll have to focus on the other person, the conversation, and your own communication. You have to make up your mind to use this approach consciously and deliberately. Keep your new focus on common ground connections in the back of your mind, especially in real time when you're having a conversation. Over time, you'll learn the best ways that will help you create common ground connections that work for you with each person with whom you talk.

6. Success factors: personal perspectives and your mind

As you increase your use of the common ground connections approach, there are personal and mental factors that will help you in that application.

(1) **Personal perspectives**
(2) **Utilizing your mind**
    (1) **Personal perspectives**
       • **Deal with personal apprehension**
        If you're introverted when communicating with others, opening up in conversations may be challenging for you. You may equate seeking common ground connections with some level of intimacy. If you're uncomfortable with that, you may be tempted to steer clear of even trying.

In reality, while seeking common ground connections may require a more personal focus from both people, it also provides more personal support from each. When you seek to create a common ground connection with another person, you're not alone. You're linked to that person. They end up wanting to create common ground connections with you. You mutually support one another.

As you begin to open up to others, you'll feel more comfortable communicating in this increasingly personal way. Because this approach "feels" so good, you'll be motivated to keep trying too.

- **Focus on others**

   When seeking common ground connections what you're really saying is: "In every conversation, I'm going to really focus on the other person with whom I'm talking." It has to be this way because common ground connections are only possible when two people are able to gather information about the other person from the conversation.

   This enhanced focus means that you must value others enough to really listen and try to understand their perspective. You focus on the other person at least as much as you do on yourself. You must value others enough to put in the effort to do this.

   It's important to accept that you don't know the complete "stories" of other people—no matter how much you believe you do. People can change and are unpredictable. Be open to learning something new and even being surprised by someone you think you know.

- **Be honest**

   Be yourself. Common ground connections only work if you and your conversational partner are honest with each other in every conversation. If you're trying to be someone you aren't, or you're trying to present an "ideal" image of yourself that isn't real, common ground connections won't happen. Any common ground connections formed in these instances will be based on inaccurate information about one or both conversational partners.

- **Learn to develop a basic interest in others**

   If you want to create more common ground connections in your conversations, you need to be generally interested in "others." Do you find "people" in general interesting? Do you enjoy having conversations with others? If you don't like "people" in general, it's going to be difficult to communicate with anyone. If you're going to realize the benefits of creating common ground connections, you have to value people and what they have to say.

- **Take responsibility for your communication**

   When you partner with others through the creation of common ground connections, you have to take responsibility for the effectiveness of your side of the conversation. Just because you thought you communicated something to the other person doesn't mean they "got it" or understood what you said. Accept responsibility for helping the other person understand.

2. **Utilizing your mind**
   - **Tap into the power of your mind**

     Our brains have an almost unlimited capacity to process information. We don't always tap into that resource in our communication, however. You have to learn to "actively" think about the conversation in which you're engaged. It also requires all parties to use their mind and observations to be flexible and adaptable in using common ground connection skills along with their existing communication skills.

     With close friends, we often get into communication "ruts." That is, we talk with them so much that we often communicate without thinking too much about it. The problem with this illusion of communication effectiveness is that the skills you used a month ago aren't really the skills you may need now. If I've been friends with Jim since high school, I may assume that I've got him all figured out. The problem with this is that Jim is constantly changing in terms of ideas and experiences based on recent events in his life. For example, Jim got married 3 months ago. If I use the same old communication skills I've always used, I may miss out on what Jim's experiencing now.

   - **Bring more of your communication to conscious awareness**

     The vast majority of our communication is unconscious or automatic. We often don't think much about it. Sometimes that works for us, sometimes not. If you want to establish common ground connections, you have to bring more of your communication to conscious awareness. This approach requires you to think actively during every conversation in order to focus on the other person and process the information necessary to connect with them.

     Keeping your communication conscious is a mental balancing act. You have to listen to the other person, listen to yourself, and process the information in the conversation. You have the mental capacity to do this, but it still requires an effort on your part to stay "active."

7. Overall benefits of creating common ground connections

The common ground connections approach can provide tremendous benefits for you in communicating with others. Consider just the following three benefits that you're likely to realize:

(1) **"Feeling" benefits of common ground connections**
(2) **Conversational benefits**
(3) **Relationship benefits**

(1) "Feeling" benefits of common ground connections

Establishing a common ground connection with someone can be difficult to define. It might be a feeling, a thought, or a sense that something special is happening between you and your conversational partner. But that "feeling" is real. You probably will have an overall positive feeling about the other person and the conversation. However, you don't necessarily need to identify "what" it is to have those good feelings.

Of course, there are times when someone with whom you're talking is sharing a sad experience. You'll still be achieving a common ground connection, but the atmosphere of the conversation may not "feel good" in that sense. Achieving common ground connections in this case is showing the person going through the problem situation that you care enough to listen.

(2) Conversational benefits

Consider the following conversational benefits that you may realize:

Finding a mutually beneficial conversational "space"

Understand that communication is an "interpersonal" endeavor. Communication involves two people seeking to understand one another. They seek that understanding in an interpersonal space which they create together. Utilizing the common ground connections approach helps you "find" that space with the other person and then communicate within it.

Understanding the "real" issue

When people are entrenched in their opinions, a given issue can be very emotional for each of them. People don't want to always give up on their side of an issue. In these cases, it becomes more important to "win" than reach a common understanding.

When you utilize common ground connections, you give up your need to "win" for the bigger reward of communicating with more understanding and more effectiveness. Both people begin to see and understand the perspectives of the other person with less chance of emotion and anger clouding the issue.

If people in the United States and the world on various sides of an issue could put aside their emotions on a given issue, they might find that they're not really in as much disagreement as they thought. They might find that there's really only a single issue on which they disagree. And even that single issue may be solvable. But often they aren't able to come to that realization. Seeking common ground connections will help with that.

(3) Relationship benefits

Using the common ground connections approach in your future conversations will help you build close relationships with others. How does that work? Consider the following benefits:

People will appreciate your efforts

Trying to establish common ground connections with others shows them that you're sincerely interested in them. People appreciate that. When you do this, you get to witness a tremendous source of appreciation that people show when they're listened to. You make other people feel good about themselves and the conversation. And they'll generally reciprocate.

You'll build more trust with others

When you start creating common ground connections in all your conversations, you get closer to others through your communication. Your focus on the other person helps break down barriers. Over time, they learn to trust you too.

Your close relationships will get "closer"

Can you strengthen common ground connections with people you know well? Definitely. Even with people you've known a long time including family and friends, you can always realize a greater closeness. When you think about it, you're always learning something new about those with whom you're closest. In most cases, your common ground connections build over the life of a relationship.

In some cases, however, the closeness of a relationship might get in the way of mutual understanding. You might think you have a "natural" common ground connection with a close friend or spouse, for example, which you've established over the history of that relationship. You know them and have a history with them it's true, but that isn't always a good thing. For example, you may not have the same patience and empathy as someone you don't know. You may feel more comfortable challenging them or their ideas than you would with someone who's a complete stranger.

In addition, some of your relationship histories might not be good. Past disagreements and problems can easily re-assert themselves in any given conversation. And remembering those past incidents may bring up strong negative emotions and diminish your attempts to understand them.

What this means is that you have to stay aware of the need to establish common ground connections on an ongoing basis in even your closest relationships. If you have a relationship "hiccup," for example, you may need to reset the relationship through the establishment of new or revised common ground connections. That is, you may be able to re-establish the things you had in common when you first became friends or first got to know them.

In other words, common ground connections aren't necessarily permanent. The factors that originally created your common ground connections can change over time. Sometimes, your relationship with another person grows closer, remains stable, or just ends through no one's fault.

8. It's not always as easy as it seems

It would seem that creating common ground connections with others would be easy most of the time. After all, who doesn't want to find things they have in common with people? Who doesn't want to feel a close connection with another person? What's more, we've all had the experience of achieving common ground connections. We know it feels good and results in more personable and effective conversations. If we focus and work at it, we should be able to recreate that experience again. There's no downside to creating common ground connections in every one of our conversations regardless of how inconsequential the conversation is. Everyone comes out ahead.

Unfortunately, it may not be as easy as it seems. Some conversations are just that—regular conversations. They don't result in an increased closeness or understanding of another person. When you pass a neighbor at the shopping center you know, for example, you say "hi." They usually say "hi" back. This is basic social convention. In this case, you're just acknowledging your relationship as a neighbor with them. Or telling a friend about a new restaurant you found this morning for breakfast may be great, but basically you're just sharing information with them. It isn't necessarily earth-shattering. Often our conversations are just "ordinary." They're still good experiences, but they're not about some deep link with another person. This can be true with even your closest friends or even your spouse.

In other cases particularly with people you don't know that well, you simply may not have that much in common with them. You and the other person may try, but sometimes similar interests just aren't there. You like them and enjoy communicating with them, but you may never establish a common ground connection. And that's fine. We need a range of relationships in our lives.

Even with people you know well like a "good" friend, your relationship with that person may not be that close. You generally might not get into "heavy" discussions with them about your innermost thoughts and fears. That's okay too.

9. Best situations to use common ground connections

Common ground connections will help you to increase the effectiveness of your communication. This is measured by increased understanding of others and an overall more positive feeling about the communication situation. This approach will also be particularly helpful in the following situations:

(1) **When you communication isn't going well.** Think about what's happening when you have conflicts, misunderstandings, or just times when you can't understand another person. Particularly with people with whom you disagree, finding common ground connections will help you communicate with those people. You may have tried various things to fix the communication problems in those relationships without success. The common ground connection approach may provide you with the answers for which you've been looking.

(2) **When disagreements are serious.** When you vehemently disagree with another person or find them offensive, common ground connections may be your only hope in just basically talking with them. You can walk away or end the relationship, but there are times when you can't do that.

(3) **When you want to increase the closeness in a relationship.** You may have a number of close relationships in your life—a wife, husband, partner, family member, friend, and many others. You enjoy your relationships with those people. You'd like to get even closer to them. However, you just don't know how.

One way to achieve an even greater degree of intimacy with another person is by using the common ground connections approach. You're working together to increase the connection you already have.

10. When common ground connections don't work

Seeking common ground connections with others doesn't always work. For example, each person has to want to "hook up" with the other person. If one or both conversational partners don't want to communicate more personally, it just won't happen. Not everyone is comfortable opening themselves up in a given conversation.

Personal challenges

Remember that when you try to change your communication, it won't always go as planned. You're modifying your communication and seeking to connect at a deeper level than you may be used to. This is an adjustment that will require you to be patient with yourself. You'll find that this effort will be well worth it, however, as you begin to communicate more clearly and in a way that will be more meaningful for you and the other person.

And keep in mind the details of how to use common ground connections approach are slightly unique to each person. Each person has to find the best ways to use the skills of the common ground connections approach with their existing skills to enhance their conversations.

11. *Can one person change the world?*

Can one person really change the world, in this case the communication between people? Will changing your communication really have any impact on healing a divided country and world? You may believe that you can't really make a difference in your country and the world just by communicating differently.

One perspective says you can. According to what's called the "butterfly effect," small actions and behaviors can have a significant impact on our world in ways we might not have originally thought possible (Gaiman & Pratchett, 2006). The butterfly effect was first proposed by meteorologist Edward Lorenz in predicting weather. The famous example is: "Does the flap of a butterfly's wings in Brazil set off a tornado in Texas?" Lorenz didn't necessarily answer this question "yes" but rather used this analogy to show that small changes in initial conditions produced large changes in long-term outcomes (Lorenz, 1969).

When we start enhancing our communication in our day-to-day lives by trying to use the common ground connections approach, we become the "butterfly." It starts with creating common ground connections with your immediate circle of friends, family, and work colleagues. Like the butterfly effect, it then can spread to your community, state, country, and maybe the world. Everything we do and think affects the people in our lives, and their reactions in turn affect others with an endless stream of possible outcomes.

Where do we start? Maybe you stop spreading gossip at work or school. This encourages others to quit as well and the target person to feel better about themselves (Flintoff, June 30, 2013). Or maybe you make a renewed effort to really listen to your uncle with whom you've never gotten along. This in turn creates a better Thanksgiving dinner for all your family. You can imagine many other communication situations in your life in which a small change on your part might make a big difference.

Making these changes is particularly important with others with whom you disagree. When you use the skills of common ground connection, you begin to break down barriers of misunderstanding and distrust. You may begin to see that people aren't as entrenched in their beliefs as you originally thought. You begin to see the world in part as they do. You don't have to agree with them, but at least you begin to understand them.

Common ground connections may not change the way different groups in the United States and the world communicate with each other overnight. This isn't the panacea to all our problems, but it's one of many things we can do to help people come together. It's a start. All change happens with a first step in a different direction. Hopefully, this book will help people take that first step.

Bibliography

Adamec, S., & Kendall-Taylor, N. (2021, January 20). Commentary: America is not as divided as you think. Yes, really. *WBUR Radio/Cognoscenti*.

Attanasio, C. (2021, October 15). Researchers asked people about worldwide divisiveness. Guess where U.S. ranked? *Los Angeles Times*.

BBC Global Survey. (2018). *A world divided.* Ipsos MORI Social Research Institute.

Cillizza, C. (2021, September 10). We're all just so damn angry. *CNN.*

Decline in Human Empathy Creates Global Risks in the 'Age of Anger.' (2019, April 8). Zurich.

Dimock, M., & Wike, R. (2020, November 13). America is exceptional in the nature of its political divide. *Pew Research Institute.*

Doherty, C., & Kiley, J. (2016, June 22). Key facts about partisanship and political animosity in America. *Pew Research Center.*

Duffy, B., & Gottfried, G. (2018). *BBC global survey: A world divided.* Ipsos MORI Research Institute.

Dunn, A., Kiley, J., Scheller, A., Baronavski, C., & Doherty, C. (2020, December 17). Voters say those on the other side "don't get" them. Here's what they want them to know. *Pew Research Center.*

Flintoff, J.-P. (2013, June 30). 198 ways to change the world. *HuffPost.*

Gaiman, N., & Pratchett, T. (2006). *Good omens: The nice and accurate prophecies of Agnes Nutter, witch.* William Morrow.

Hobcroft, C. (2017, March 21). Connecting with people—what it is and isn't, and why you might find it hard. *Harley Therapy Counseling Blog.*

Hobson, K. (2018). *Clicking: How our brains are in sync.* Alumni Weekly.

Horowitz, J. M. (2019, May 8). Americans see advantages and challenges in country's growing racial and ethnic diversity. *Pew Research Center.*

Khairzada, Z. (2020, July 2). Strangers find common ground by 'not focusing on the differences.' *Spectrum News 1.*

Lardieri, A. (2018, April 25). People around the world feel more divided than they did 10 years ago. *U.S. News and World Report.*

Lorenz, E. N. (1969). Three approaches to atmospheric predictability. *Bulletin of the American Meteorological Society, 50,* 345–349.

Lowery, T. (2022, April 1). 10 heartbreaking facts about ongoing conflicts around the world. *Global Citizen.*

Method Communications (2021, October 27). Is empathy dead in America? *Cision, PR Newswire.*

Ng, S. (2017, March 21). How do I know if I'm really connecting to others? *Harley Therapy Counseling Blog.*

Poushter, J., & Fetterolf, J. (2019, April 22). How people around the world view diversity in their countries. *Pew Research Center.*

Poushter, J., & Kent, N. (2020, June 25). The global divided on homosexuality persists. *Pew Research Center.*

Public Agenda/USA Today/Ipsos. (2021, April 27). Nine in ten Americans say overcoming divisiveness is now more important than ever. *Public Agenda/USA Today/Ipsos.*

Seppala, E. M. (2012, August 26). Social connection improves health, well-being, and longevity. Feeling it. *Psychology Today.*

Wazir, Z. (2021, June 23). People see more social division after pandemic. *U.S. News and World Reports.*

Yudkin, D. A., Hawkins, S., & Dixon, T. (2019, September 14). The perception gap: How false impressions are pulling Americans apart. *PsyArXiv.*

2

RESOLVING CONFLICT

There will always be conflicts and disagreements with the people with whom you communicate even those with whom you're closest. This is because to a certain extent we all live in separate worlds. We can't completely understand another person's world nor can they understand ours. This can be true even with the members of your family, a friend with whom you grew up, or really anyone with whom you communicate.

Certainly, in conflict situations communication has "broken down" for some reason. You can't necessarily figure out how to fix it. And it's no wonder. Conflict

DOI:10.4324/9781003357049-2

between people is complex. Consider just the following factors involved in conflict situations:

1. **People don't always listen well to one another.**
   Studies show that people can listen sometimes with only a 25% efficiency.
2. **There are multiple perspectives held by two people in a given conversation—not just one perspective per person.**
   People can even change their perspectives within the same conversation.
3. **Two people can understand the same topic in a conversation in a completely different way.**
4. **Conflict can often involve strong emotions.**
   Emotions and particularly anger can cloud the thinking of both people.
5. **People often feel like they must "defend" what they say in a conversation.**
   This occurs even if what they stated earlier in a conversation was really just information they wanted to randomly share. It really wasn't their opinion or even something in which they strongly believed.
6. **The "type" of relationship can drastically affect the conflict.**

In close relationships, for example, conflict is usually different from conflict with a co-worker or acquaintance. Conflict can be more emotional and intense in a marriage because both parties have made a long-term investment, care about the health of the relationship, and thus are intensely interested in every conversation that doesn't go well.

In contrast, you may not be that close to a co-worker. You may not know them that well because you haven't worked on any projects together. You have less invested and may be limited by the restrictions of the workplace to get too upset.

Your efforts in bringing your world together through your use of common ground connection skills can be motivated by the realization that other people share your perspective. There are still people who are willing to try to understand other people and groups. We often make assumptions about the United States and the world based on the loudest angry people, but there are still reasoned folks who appreciate the value of each person and their opinions. There is hope, but we need to start working on our conflict now before it gets any worse.

Conflict in America

There is clearly a perception in the United States that people live in a divided nation. A majority of Americans say there are strong political, racial, and ethnic conflicts (Bailey & Elbeshbishi, 2021).

What's worse is that 30% of Americans believe people in the United States don't even know how to talk about their disagreements in constructive ways (Ipsos, 2021). Because of this inability or unwillingness to be open to other perspectives, people get angry when others don't agree with them. They can't believe the other group believes what they do. Taken further they can't even agree on the "facts" of an issue. Based on this inflexibility differences are becoming "personal."

Impacting every person

Areas of division and conflict have begun to filter down to the everyday lives of each American too. Consider the following results from a 2021 Ipsos poll (Ipsos, 2021):

- Seven out of 10 Americans say they have often or sometimes avoided talking about politics with someone whose political views are opposed to their own in the last 12 months.
- About two-thirds of people surveyed said they have often thought someone else was being too sensitive and defensive about politics.
- One-fourth of Americans say they've even ended relationships with someone because of differing views.

In addition, research shows that partisan polarization and divisiveness in America are increasingly filtering down to individual citizens. Specifically, divisiveness is contributing to the development of anxiety, depression, and sleep disorders (Nayak et al., 2021). The extent of differences is contributing to general mental health problems as well (Montoya-Williams & Fuentes-Afflick, 2019).

Americans believe that divisiveness in the country is driven by national leaders, social media, and the news media. These sources have exacerbated existing divisions in the country (Hidden Common Ground, 2020). Americans believe that the focus in America should be more on common ground and less on political hostility (Ipsos, 2021).

Conflict in the world

There are at least 27 active conflicts in the world today. Conflicts in Ukraine, Afghanistan, Yemen, Myanmar, Ethiopia, and political instability in Lebanon are getting worse (Lowery, 2022; Council on Foreign Relations, Global Conflict Tracker, 2022). The reasons for these conflicts range from territorial disputes and regional tensions to corruption. Millions are killed or displaced from their homes. Basic services like food and water become unavailable as people are forced into extreme poverty.

Globally, conflict and violence are on the rise, according to the United Nations. The United Nations has warned that peace is **more** under threat than it has been since World War II. 274 million people globally live in conflict-affected areas. Organized crime, urban and domestic violence, and violent extremism are all part of the current state of conflict in the world also.

This is the situation the world finds itself in today. The current humanitarian crisis in Ukraine may be in the spotlight in 2022, but there are many conflicts occurring globally that deserve equal attention and compassion.

When the world is divided

When the world is divided as it is, conflict is both the cause and the continuation of the many divisions. Over the last few years, it's obvious that many people have become more angry and entrenched in their beliefs. Some have begun to perceive others who disagree with them as not only wrong but also evil. When you adopt this "you're evil if you don't agree with me" perspective, you perpetuate divisions and disagreements.

When you're so convinced of the "rightness" of your beliefs, you may try to "force" others to believe what you believe. You can force people in a number of ways including using your standing as a manager in business, belittling friends and family who disagree with you, insulting a person who may be your friend, or in many other subtle and not-so-subtle ways. You're not so much forcing someone to do something as much as you're attempting to intimidate them to change their beliefs to agree with you. You show in this way that you don't have much respect for their perspective or them as a person. People don't like being strong armed in this way.

When you attempt to intimidate or force people to believe or do something, you often experience what is called the "backlash" effect. When you "push on" people to try to force them to change their point of view, people will sometimes dig in their heels and refuse to even listen to you. By trying to force someone to adopt your perspective, you're really hurting your case. People are best persuaded when you start with them and what they believe. You then attempt in a respectful way to move them closer to your point of view.

People who are forced to believe something aren't persuaded anyway, they're coerced. You may never get someone to really change their beliefs. And even if they do, new beliefs that are coerced in this manner rarely last. People will generally go back to their original position once the coercion is removed.

Table of contents

1. Resolving conflict starts with each one of us

Changing the conflict in the world starts with each one of us. Where do we start to make a difference? We can start with our friends, family, work colleagues, and communities. Maybe you "make peace" with a person at work with whom you've never gotten along. Or perhaps you reach out to Aunt Cheryl by visiting and talking with her about a big argument you had with her last year.

But you may ask yourself: "Can one person really make a difference?" You can through your communication with others. When you communicate using the common ground connections approach, you change your communication and the communication in the conversation. You start a movement of communication change which extends outward from you to others in your community. If enough people change their communication in this way, the world can be changed (Inspire Kindness, 2022).

2. The nature of conflict

It will help you in seeking common ground connections, if you understand the nature of conflict itself. There are important parts of your thinking, feelings, and personality that helps to explain why you react to conflict the way you do.

Anger

Anger becomes part of a conflict situation for a number of reasons. Anger can be the result of a threat to your ego. Someone says something that is critical of you in some way. You believe they're attacking a part of who you are. Anger becomes a logical defense mechanism. It can even lead to wanting to enact revenge on that person in some way.

You can also just feel very passionately about an issue. You want everyone to agree with you. When they don't you get frustrated and angry.

Anger will also distract you from using aspects of the common ground connections approach. The approach requires that you really think about the conversation while it's occurring. Sometimes, when you're angry you aren't thinking clearly. Extreme emotions can cloud your thinking. At the moment, you might say anything that pops into your head (which you may regret later).

Desperation

If your anger and frustration are great enough, you may get desperate. You're thinking is: "I must convince them. I must get them to accept my view of the situation no matter what." Thus, you may resort to any means to convince the other person including:

- telling lies
- verbally attacking them
- spreading rumors
- attacking them physically

These and other responses of angry desperation seem to be happening more and more within our country and the world. We've let our opinions become ingrained and inflexible to any kind of change. When your ingrained opinions are challenged, you face a fear that the basis for your life is being called into question. This can create desperate feelings which block you from dealing with the situation rationally.

Desperate people are just that too—desperate. When you're desperate you may do anything to resolve a situation. This has included violence between groups within our country. The thinking is: "I don't know what else to do to convince another person or group so I'll try to violently force them to believe the way I do" or "I don't want those people in my life or my society. I need to remove them from my life."

Anxiety

Running through all of the previous factors are your personal feelings of anxiety. Anxiety is always involved to some extent in conflict situations. If you're anxious, you may be thinking more about your anxiety than about what you're going to say next, the other person, or the conversation itself. It affects the soundness of your thinking.

Research has shown that anxiety will cause you to fit in what the other person is saying into your existing perspectives. It may limit your capacity to acquire a fresh perspective, learn anything new, or even listen effectively (Sillars et al., 2001).

Your anxiety often causes you to want to resolve the conflict quickly by any means necessary rather than take the time to really solve the problem. If someone says to you, "Oh, Cheryl and I always argue about the same things." What this really means is perhaps you and Cheryl need to step back and really examine what's been going on between the two of you, and solve the issue once and for all.

3. Establishing common ground

One of the most important actions you can take when you're having an argument with someone is to find common ground with them. That is, try to focus at least as much time on what you have in common as on how you differ.

Our default action in conflict situations is often to defend our position without considering that the other person may have a valid point of view. We do that especially in those times when the issue being contested generates anger and frustration within us.

The following points may help you in successfully establishing common ground real time in a conversation.

Bond over less-polarized issues

In other words, before tackling the toughest issue between you and the other person, work to achieve common ground on issues in which there is a lower level of disagreement. Maybe you could both agree on the problems with the United States economy before tackling the January 6, 2022 attack on the capitol, for example.

Be open to taking the time to listen and understand the viewpoints of others

Ask questions to clarify the other person's opinion (Duchovnay et al., 2020). Exchange feedback.

When you seek common ground in conflict situations, you're working to detail the issues that you and your conversational partner disagree on. In order to deal with the situation, each person must consider and prioritize all areas of possible disagreement. You're also seeking to make sure your partner correctly understands your perspective.

4. Seek "connections" in conflict situations

As you seek common ground, you can then go deeper to establish a connection with the other person.

Guidelines for achieving a "connection" with another person in conflict situations include the following.

(1) Be patient

It may take some time to drill down on the aspects of common ground you've found with someone in order to establish a connection. You're seeking to detail their perspective. You'll need to try different questions and prompts. Some of those will work. Some won't. Their perspective may be so different from your own that it may take some time to really understand what they believe.

(2) Listen intently to what the other person is sharing

Put extra energy into picking up as much information as possible to understand the other person's perspective completely.

(3) Stay mentally energized throughout the conversation

This will help you listen to what the other person is saying, process the information, and then respond appropriately and in such a way that you build a bond with that person.

5. Combining common ground and connections

Combining the actions of "common ground" with "connections" provides you with the advantages of "common ground connections." Be aware that you can use the common ground connections approach in any conflict situation.

6. Establishing common ground connections in real-life situations

When you're actually in a given conflict conversation trying to establish common ground connections, it will help if you keep the following points in mind.

Put in the effort to find at least one thing you have in common with the other person

In conflict situations, you may believe that you have nothing in common with the other person. But this usually isn't the situation in most conflicts. Generally one or at most two real, core arguments that need to be addressed. There may be other issues involved, but they don't need to be addressed first.

Keep in mind that sometimes arguments are just two people who aren't communicating very well. We're not communicating our point of view in such a way that the other person can understand. Make sure you examine the communication taking place in terms of both people.

Seek to get to know to person with whom you're having a conflict

Why do they believe as they do? What's their background? People are usually willing to share their lives with others who show an interest. They'll appreciate at a minimum you're trying to understand them as a person. As you get to know someone, you'll be able to use that information to connect and get close to that person. This connection should result in an easier resolution of disagreements.

Continue to use the actions of common ground connections throughout the conversation

Don't give up if you face resistance or you think that what you're doing isn't working. Build on any commonalities you establish with that person.

When we seek mutual understanding in a conversation, it helps to build the "relationship" part of the conversation. When you are talking to someone, you're in relationship with them. You've agreed to interact with them as one person to another. This means you temporarily form a relationship with them so you can communicate more effectively. It may not be a relationship as in a friend or work colleague, but it's still a relationship. Because of this relationship aspect, people are usually more willing to play fair, be open, and engage equally in that conversation.

There may be instances in which you may be "stuck" in terms of dealing with conflict. You may have tried many things without changing the situation much. Utilizing common ground connections can provide you with new perspectives that may help you resolve even the most intractable conflict situations.

7. Serious conflict

How about the instance in which the conflict you're having with another person has grown to be serious or even threatening to one or both people? Can the common ground connections approach help in this situation as much as in a "regular" conversation?

When conflict moves to a situation in which the disagreement is serious, common ground connections can sometimes be your last hope. A serious disagreement is one in which one or both people have tried numerous things without success to resolve the conflict. You're becoming increasingly frustrated and angry with the person and the situation. They're apparently feeling the same way.

Maybe you need to walk away and deal with it later. But it could be someone with whom you have to work with or a person in your family with whom you have to communicate with daily. And if you operate from a position of hope believing that you can communicate with anyone, you may not want to give up.

So what can you do? In addition to following the previous common ground connection actions, you must really open up your thinking. Work hard to let them talk even if you want to break into what they're saying because you disagree with them or are offended by what they're saying. Put your own thoughts on hold for the moment. Your new goal in the conversation is to gather information about them and their position and to hold off judging them until you have more information.

8. Violent conflict

Will the common ground connections approach work in potentially violent situations? What do you do if you feel an individual or group might use physical aggression or violence to back up what they say? What should you do if you fear for your safety because of your race, religion, lifestyle, or beliefs? Will the common ground connections approach work in these potentially violent situations?

First of all, if you really believe you're in danger, leave the situation. If, for example, you're openly gay, and you're faced with people who are clearly anti-gay, what should you do? Given that they want to beat you up or even kill you, the best thing is to leave the situation. Get help by any means necessary.

Second, you may want to avoid such situations in the future. It may restrict your freedom, but sometimes it's best to live to fight another day. Address the issue in another way.

Third, if you're a fit, strong person you may be tempted to use physical force yourself. Meeting their force with more force won't solve the problem. This is true because by the time you get to that point the differences are so pronounced a one-time fistfight will only make things worse. And if you take the conflict to the "next level" by using guns, bats, knives, or other weapons you may find yourself in jail.

9. How do you "think about" conflict?

Conscious processes

People interpret conflict situations in a way that makes sense to them. This is often done without thinking too much about how the other person in the conversation is interpreting the same information. This lack of focus is the reason two people can draw completely different conclusions from the same conversation.

To help you best deal with conflict situations, you must keep the conversation as conscious as possible. Keep the common ground connections approach at the forefront of your mind in every conversation. This will allow you to stay more engaged and look for any opportunities to link up with the other person. It will guide you in focusing on why you're having a conflict with them and how to resolve that conflict.

Unconscious processes

Unconscious mental processes are best demonstrated by the fact that people tend to use the same way to deal with and try to resolve conflict from one conversation to another without much thought (Canary et al., 2001). You've learned what works for you so you use a conflict approach you've had success with in the past. Unfortunately, this doesn't always work because conflict can be a very different problem from conversation to conversation. A different conflict strategy may be needed for each unique conversation.

Conscious and unconscious processes in practice

If you want to be effective in creating common ground connections, you must examine your conscious and unconscious thinking in every conversation. The following points will help you do that:

> **Stay aware of your own emotions.** Particularly in conflict situations in which you might get angry, creating an 'awareness of your thinking is key. All of us have what's called a "natural mimic reflex" or "negative emotional spiral." These reflexes and downward spirals occur when both sides escalate the conflict, say hurtful things or even make threats. You raise your negative emotions to match your partner's. When someone starts yelling at you, you're likely to yell back. Your goal is to stay "one up" on the other person. The longer this goes, the less likely the situation is going to be resolved successfully.
>
> By staying aware of your emotions you can immediately recognize when you're getting too angry or upset. If for example you feel like throwing something, or pounding a table, you're probably getting too emotional and angry. Pause or just listen without interrupting the other person. Think through what's going on and how you're contributing to the situation. If you're focused on only preparing an argument against them, you won't be able to really listen to their side of the issue in real-time.
>
> **Sometimes walk away.** If you determine by thinking through the situation that you are in fact too angry or emotional, it's sometimes best to

excuse yourself and walk away. Knowing when to walk away or postpone a conflict conversation can be just as critical as knowing when to continue that conversation. (Brett, 2014). If you decide to walk away, it's best to let the other person know why you're leaving. You might say something like: "I'm really too angry now by all this. I'm going back to my desk and try to clear my head. Maybe we can meet tomorrow to talk about this further." Take responsibility for the end of the conversation. Just let the other person know that you would like to continue the conversation at some future time.

If after thinking about it, you feel the person is irrational, you may conclude that you don't really want to deal with the situation. If this is the case, you'll want to think about whether you want to interact with that person again. But if you decide to try again, a break might give you a chance to develop a strategy for the next conversation.

10. Communicating with people with whom we have conflict

Changing our communication through common ground connections will inevitably be put to the test when individuals and groups with the strongest differences begin talking to one another. We'll have to use this approach even with groups we find the most radical and hateful. The idea is to create a new communication atmosphere where people have tolerance, understanding, empathy, and respect for one another.

With people with whom you disagree, the common ground connections approach is just saying before getting into a yelling and screaming match with a person with whom you disagree, start by just talking with them as one human being to another. Get to know them at a basic level. Find out "who they are really." Before you even get into arguing about things you disagree with, see what you have in common with them. Everyone has at least one thing in common with a given person even those people that frankly you find offensive.

When we think about talking with people or groups with whom we disagree, we all have a tendency to avoid the conversation. The question we often ask is: "Why would I even want to talk with this person? They aren't worth my time."

So why is it worth your time? Consider just the following:

It will make your own life better. You'll begin to understand other people's perspectives better.

Your conflicts will be fewer. You'll have more peace in your life by learning to interact with more people.

Your community, the country, and the world will be better. We all contribute to the communication atmosphere. Solving the issues of divisiveness and disagreement currently in our world is up to each one of us. It starts with everyone's individual lives and can move out from there. People will feel good about themselves, their relationships, and ultimately everyone in the world.

11. Communicating in extreme conflict situations

How can the common ground connections approach help in extreme conflict situations?

Seek common ground connections first

This approach requires that people first find common ground and go further to seek more personal connections. Combining these skills that every person already has is powerful in bringing people together. People begin to understand one another better. When you start with commonalities and ways we are similar people will disagree less and certainly when they do disagree will do so with less anger. Common ground connections are one solution to the situation currently in our country.

Work hard to focus on the other person regardless of your level of disagreement with them

The common ground connections approach also requires that individuals focus on the other person more than they may be used to. When you do this, you begin to understand others, particularly those people with whom you don't agree or don't like. You might have previously created a really negative impression of a person because of the group with which they identified or them personally.

Hear people out

This approach asks you to hear people out regardless of how much you disagree with them. You must put your own agenda on hold as you listen to them. You must check your emotional reactions to what the other person says so you can think clearly.

Simply put, we agree more than we think we do. It may be time to start talking about what unites not divides the world.

12. Don't ignore real differences

Sometimes there are "real" differences between two people. Sometimes, you're just not going to agree with another person (Mipham, 2017).

13. Impossible connections

Realistically, are there some people with whom you can't create a common ground connection? Although hope springs eternal, there may be some people you just can't reach. And some people don't want to listen to you or anyone else who doesn't agree with them. They've made up their minds and that's it.

14. People are making a difference

At the first glance, it may appear that the divisiveness and conflict in the world are pervasive. But, if we stand back and look at this environment from an individual perspective, we may not be as divided as we think. Do you have real differences with your friends? Sometimes, but not always. Do you have conflicts with the grocery store clerk? Usually not. How about the mechanic who fixes your car? You might differ on the price of repairs but probably not the mechanic as a person. Everyone works together and communicates pretty well most of the time. If a person from Nashville, Tennessee, traveled to California and met a person at a restaurant in Santa Monica, they probably would have a perfectly reasonable discussion despite differences. That would hold true for two people from any part of the world. One-on-one we don't seem that different.

We need to start assuming that even the people with whom we disagree the most hold views that are based on good intentions. Each person in this country cares about their families, neighbors, communities, and the health of the world. They often just have different beliefs than we do.

The evidence seems to suggest that people have at least a perception of their country and the world as divided on a significant number of issues. But to what extent is that true?

Often the loudest, most divisive voices are the only ones that are heard, and they represent a small segment of a given population. The largest number of people in every society hold a more moderate view of the world and have hope for a more united future. Consider the following actions being taken by citizens in the United States which show a desire to unify.

World kindness movements

The "be kind" movements in the United States are examples of people's realization that we've become too much of an angry, divided country. World kindness movements include organizations such as envision kindness, kindness.org, world kindness USA, the be kind people project, and the Kind Campaign. These movements are making a difference.

Volunteerism

Consider the number of people who volunteer within the United States in comparison to the claim that "we're divided." According to the Corporation for

National and Community Service, over 25% or 62.8 million Americans volunteer each year. They donate 7.9 billion hours of service or the equivalent of $184 billion per year. These volunteers come from all racial or ethnic groups, ages, and wealth levels. They serve on town and city boards, school boards, and in many other capacities. A divided country doesn't have this many people volunteering to help others.

Community support

Local businesses in most communities support schools by sponsoring various sports teams. All they want is "Chuck's Plumbing" on the back of the school's baseball uniforms. Community members coach local sports teams. Area churches work within their cities to help those who are homeless.

Political bipartisanship

Even political parties particularly at the local level are working together to make positive changes in America. Take the following examples of how people and politicians are working across divides to make a positive impact in their communities.

American public square

This Kansas City-based community organization works to improve the tone and quality of public discourse by (1) convening groups for respectful topics on important topics in the community, (2) educating the community about how to engage the community in an effective way, and (3) engaging diverse segments of the community to ensure multiple perspectives are explored (Brooks, 2022).

Living room conversations

This group seeks to connect people across divides—politics, age, gender, race, nationality, and more—through guided conversations proven to build understanding and transform communities. These conversations occur throughout the United States (Keefe, 2022).

People in the United States and the world are starting to realize that conflict in the world needs to be addressed. They're beginning at a local level to "push back" against this perception of a divided world by making real efforts. There are definite indications that at an individual and local community level, we're as unified as ever. It may be all in how you look at it.

Bibliography

Bailey, P. M., & Elbeshbishi, S. (2021, April 27). Hidden common ground poll: Americans want compromised but think political gridlock will worsen. *USA Today*.

Brennan Center for Justice. (2022, May 26). Voting rights roundup.

Brett, J. (2014, June 10). When and how to let a conflict go. *Harvard Business Review*.

Burgoon, J. K., Berger, C. R., & Waldron, V. R. (2000). Mindfulness and interpersonal communication. *Journal of Social Issues, 56*(1), 105–127. https://doi.org/10.1111/0022-4537.0015 4

Canary, D. J., Cupach, W. R., & Serpe, R. T. (February, 2011). A competence-based approach to examining interpersonal conflict: Test of a longitudinal model. *Sage Journals, 28*(1). https://doi.org/10.1177/009365001028001003

Chan, M. (2022, June 23). The supreme court just vastly expanded gun rights. Here's what happens next. *NBC News*.

Duchovnay, M., Moore, C., & Masullo, G. M. (2020, July). How to talk to people who disagree with you politically. *Center for Media Engagement*. https://mediaengagement. org/research/divided-communities.

Ely, R. J., & Thomas, D. A. (2020, November-December). Getting serious about diversity: Enough already with the business case. *Harvard Business Review*.

Haidet, J., & Rose-Stockwell, T. (2019, December). The dark psychology of social networks. *The Atlantic*.

Hartig, H. (2022, June 13). About six-in-ten Americans say abortion should be legal in all or most cases. *Pew Research Center*.

Hidden Common Ground: Challenging the Narrative of a Divided America. (2020, October 20). *USA Today*.

Hurley, L., & Chung, A. (2022, June 27). U.S. supreme court overturns Roe v. Wade, ends constitutional right to abortion. Reuters.

Inspire Kindness Team. (2022). Kindness 101: What is kindness and how do you teach it. *Inspire Kindness*.

Ipsos. (2021, December 13). Most Americans believe political hostility and divisiveness between ordinary Americans is a serious problem. *Public Agenda/USA Today/Ipsos Poll*.

Keefe, H. (2022). Love your enemies: How decent people can save America from the culture of contempt. *Church, Communication and Culture, 7*(2), 438–440. DOI: 10.1080/23753234.2022.2074488

Ledur, J., Rabinowitz, K., & Galocha, A. (2022, July 5). There have been over 300 mass shootings so far in 2022. *The Washington Post*.

Lowery, T. (2022, April 1). 10 heartbreaking facts about ongoing conflicts around the world. *Global Citizen*.

Mipham, S. (2017, November 21). How to connect and find common ground in any situation. *Better—NBC* (Excerpted from The Lost Art of Good Conversation: A Mindful Way to Connect with Others and Enrich Everyday Life by Tibetan spiritual leader, Sakyong Mipham).

Montoya-Williams, D., & Fuentes-Afflick, E. F. (2019, July 19). Political determinants of population health. *JAMA Network, 2*(7).

Nayak, S. S., Fraser, T., Panagopoulos, C., Aldrich, D., & Kim, D. (2021, September 21). Is divisive politics making Americans sick? Associations of perceived partisan polarization with physical and mental health outcomes among adults in the United States. *Social Science & Medicine*, (284).

NPR. (2022, June 27). On gun control, two big steps in opposite directions. "Consider This". *NPR*.

Pramuk, J. (2022, June 24). Congress passes most significant gun reform bill in decades, sends it to Biden. *CNBC*.

Sillars, A., Roberts, L. J., Leonard, K. E., & Dun, T. (2001). Cognition during marital conflict: The relationship of thought and talk. *Journal of Social and Personal Relationships*, *17*(4/5), 479–502.

Tensley, B. (2022). America's long history of Black voter suppression. *CNN Politics*.

Totenberg, N., & McCammon, S. (2022, June 24). Supreme court overturns Roe v Wade, ending right to abortion upheld for decades. *NPR*.

Williams, P. (2022, June 23). Supreme court allows the carrying of firearms in public in major victory for gun rights Group. *NBC News*.

3

THE UNCONSCIOUS COMMUNICATOR

Preview of chapter

1. Your physical brain
2. Conscious, preconscious, and unconscious processes
3. Speed of conscious and unconscious processing
4. How the conscious and unconscious work together
5. Awareness
6. Where does your processing start?
7. How consciousness and unconsciousness "fight each other"
8. We're not "out of control"

DOI:10.4324/9781003357049-3

As you read through this chapter, note that we don't have all the answers to how your mind works. What follows are the perspectives that seem to have the most research or in some cases intuitive support. This chapter isn't meant to be a primer on your conscious and unconscious processes. Rather the goal is to provide the most practical information in using your mind to enhance your communication skills and find common ground connections.

1. Your physical brain

Your brain has a tremendous capacity to process information. It's estimated that our brains make millions of calculations per second (Choi, 2013). But, despite this capacity, we still can't take in all that's happening around us. In fact, sometimes our brain is limited in terms of what it can do. Sometimes, our minds just can't put all the information together in a coherent way (Fahkry, 2018). You may have experienced this yourself when you felt overwhelmed by a conversation or situation. Despite using all your mental energies or how hard you "tried," you may not have been able to make sense of what the other person just said.

Limitations of your brain

1. Prioritizing: Your brain can process a huge amount of information from a conversation but has trouble prioritizing all of the information you receive. This is important because everything is competing for your brain's resources. Since you can't "take in" or pay attention to everything, deciding on what to pay attention to is important.

How do you do that? You have to "make that call" yourself in every conversation. Maybe some information shared isn't that important like where someone ate for lunch. Other information like a person relating his breakup with a girlfriend would be an area to which you should listen as closely as you can. We all develop our own set of priorities in deciding what to process. It's usually dependent upon the people involved, the topic of the conversation, and what may be happening at the time. Your most difficult job is often deciding what to ignore.

Prioritization is really important in the establishment of common ground connections because it's how you decide what communication from the other person to key in on. Those factors include the following:

1. **What you believe the other person needs from you during the conversation.** The other person for example may be relating a problem in their family. What do they need from you—empathy, just to listen, etc. **(focusing on the other person)?**
2. **What you believe will help you understand the other person in the current conversation (seeking common ground).**
3. **What information will help you really understand and create a close connection with them (common ground connections).**

Prioritization is a process that we learn. We can improve our abilities through practice.

2. It appears that we can't remember everything we take in: The word "appears" is used because we don't really know whether people take in everything they experience or not. Some research indicates that everything each of us has ever processed in our minds is stored somewhere in our brain. That research supports the idea that we don't forget information. Rather it's a "retrieval" problem. We can't pull out a particular piece of information from the recesses of our brain when we need it.

Other researchers conclude that we simply forget some things. We can't "retrieve" it because it's not there. And of course there are positions on a continuum between each of these perspectives (McLeod, 2008).

What determines what we "forget" and what we "remember?" According to a study by Daphna Shohamy (2018), our brains filter our experiences, preserving some memories and allowing others to be forgotten. She found that "information that is the most rewarding" is most likely to be retained.

What is clear is that, when you're in a conversation with someone, you're not going to remember everything the other person says (Pietrangelo, 2019). Think about the last conversation you had. You were talking, listening, reading the other person's nonverbal communication, and perhaps remembering something from the past that was related. Your mind was going a "million miles a minute."

Often it's difficult to put all this together. For example, as you were formulating a response to what the other person said, you may have stopped listening briefly. We've all been "caught" in the situation in which the other person says: "What do you think about what I just said?" Unfortunately, you weren't listening at that exact point because you were thinking about what you wanted to say next. You switch between all these conversational roles with unbelievable speed, but you still can't process everything that's going on.

3. Failure to take advantage of your thought speed advantage: Thought speed is the difference between one person's speed of talking and a second person's speed of processing the information or listening. The average person talks at about 150 words per minute. We can process information at least three times that fast (Romig, 2015). That means the listener has "extra" time in every conversation. Admittedly, this extra time can be seconds, but those seconds add up in any conversation.

Unfortunately, we don't often take advantage of this thought speed time. It may not be a concept that you've heard before and therefore are unclear on how this might help. For example, I may choose to daydream with this "extra" time instead of thinking more deeply about the conversation in which I'm engaged.

Using your thought speed is an advantage that enables you to get as much information as possible about the other person. It requires that you stay mentally active throughout a conversation. You never know when the other person may share information that you can use to create common ground connections with them. (More on your thought speed advantage in the chapter on listening.)

2. Conscious, preconscious, and unconscious processes: To "manage" all the information around us, we use three processes of our brain—preconscious, conscious, and unconscious processing.

Your preconscious mind

Preconscious memories are not the same things as memories that are readily accessed, such as remembering your way home. They are unrepressed memories that we extract for a specific purpose at a specific time (Cherry, 2020). You can call these memories to mind easily if something "triggers" your thinking. Let's say you're talking to a friend. She's talking about the unbelievable pizza she had last night at a local restaurant. You have been to the restaurant before and had a similar experience. You can almost taste the pizza (Thomas, 2022).

Your conscious mind

The conscious part of your mind is really the awareness of your own thoughts, feelings, memories, attitudes, beliefs, and sensations and the world around you in the present moment. In a sense, it creates your reality—what you understand right now. You choose which of these thoughts you want to actively hold in your mind at any given point because you can't take in everything that's going on around you. The information that isn't chosen moves to your long-term memory or is forgotten.

Your unconscious mind

People often assume that most of our mind's activity occurs in the conscious part of our mind. This is where people live day-to-day. They aren't always aware of anything else. In fact, however, there's as much or more activity in the unconscious as opposed to the conscious part of your mind.

Unconscious thoughts are more difficult to access than conscious or preconscious thoughts. Unconscious thoughts can't be remembered without extensive effort. For example, you may have had a serious car accident when you were a child that you don't like to or want to remember .

In contrast, sometimes you have a thought or memory of something that you believe comes from your unconscious that is related to your current conversation. It just seems to "pop" up out of nowhere into your consciousness. The most common example of unconscious behavior is the Freudian slip. This is where a person says something they immediately realize isn't appropriate. For example, calling your new wife by your ex-wife's name (Ricee, 2021). In other words, we have less control over our unconscious processes than over our conscious and preconscious processes (Ricee, 2021).

How does your unconscious work? Basically, your unconscious stores short- and long-term memories which help in making interpretations of things happening now. You probably remember your current phone number, but you may not remember your phone number where you grew up. Your beliefs, attitudes, and values also reside in your unconscious filtering everything you experience including your prejudices and biases.

Your unconscious mind is always "on," operating 24/7 in collecting information. It handles all your basic physical functions—breathing, digestion, and heart rate (Berg, 2018; Marra, 2021). Breathing, for example, is an automatically learned behavior. You don't think much about it unless you're exercising or meditating. If for some reason you suddenly can't breathe, however, then this usually unconscious action becomes very conscious.

Because we're not completely aware of how our unconscious works, it often feels like the information contained in the unconscious is inaccessible. But you access that information all the time. And it's a good thing, because the unconscious contains an unbelievable amount of information that you can use and need at any given moment.

Your unconscious mind is important on a number of levels. We know that sometimes your unconscious actually makes decisions for you without you consciously being aware of it. One research study by Dijksterhuis et al. (2006) even found that choices in problem situations could be based on your unconscious. His reasoning was that unconscious thought can process and draw on more information than conscious thought alone. The implication is that your unconscious may run more of your life than you realize.

3. Speed of conscious and unconscious processing: All this conscious and unconscious processing happens in fractions of a second during a conversation. Because interpersonal communication is so complex and conversations proceed so quickly, extensive deliberation is not always possible. We're involved in communication, thinking as we go, and responding almost faster than we can process the conversation. What's consciousness doing while the unconscious is doing all this work? Bargh (1997) believes that "consciousness" is floating ahead in time, setting up strategic, automatic contingencies for the future where they might be needed (novel or problematic situations). This enables us to respond fluently and appropriately in the present (p. 244)."

This doesn't always work perfectly. The unconscious part of your mind often passes along information some of which seems random and occasionally nonsensical. Sometimes, despite our best efforts we get confused.

4. How the conscious and unconscious work together: Your conscious and unconscious make up a system that helps you navigate life. They are inextricably linked with each having specific actions they normally handle individually as discussed in the previous section. But sometimes the dividing line on those responsibilities is blurred.

How does this work? The following is one conception of this mental process. Usually, consciousness is attending to the most important things in a conversation. The most important things could be determined by your own priorities, the priorities of a friend, an emergency situation, or a number of other factors.

What we choose to ignore in a given conversation is handed off to unconscious processing. According to Bargh and Chartrand (1999), unconscious processing is, in a sense, a "mental butler" who knows our tendencies, habits, and preferences.

How does the unconscious do this? Your unconscious provides your conscious with access to all the information it needs when it needs it. It filters out all the unnecessary information and delivers only that which is needed at the time. The unconscious communicates all this information into consciousness via emotions, feelings, sensations, images, and dreams. It doesn't communicate in words.

If the situation is something new, your unconscious will pull up the information it best associates with this new information to help you make sense of it. When you meet someone for the first time, for example, you may not be sure how to proceed. As you continue to talk to them, the conscious part of your mind is processing information from the conversation.

The unconscious is also helping you understand this new person by pulling up information from past similar conversations. This is the process by which each of us can determine any common ground that we have with others. In addition, this process continues to operate during a conversation as we drill down on the common ground we've found in order to establish connections with that person.

5. Awareness: Both areas of your brain are always aware at any point in time. We are often unaware of our unconscious mind, yet it exerts considerable influence over how we think, feel, and behave (Taylor, 2022).

You may have experienced this yourself. Have you ever driven to work, but when you get there you have no memory of the trip? For example, maybe you were focused on thinking about a friend of yours who was sick. In this case, your unconscious is fully aware and does the thinking necessary to drive the car while your conscious is focused on something else (in this case your friend's illness). You're not driving along half out of it. Your consciousness is still aware of what's going on at some level but is letting the unconscious handle the majority of the work. If you almost get into a wreck because someone cuts you off, your consciousness will kick in and take the lead.

In most situations, you aren't completely on automatic pilot or totally aware. Your mind is somewhere on a communication continuum between these two extremes. It switches instantaneously as needed to handle the present situation.

"Automatic Pilot"————**Total awareness of your communication**

"Where" you are on this continuum depends on such factors as:

1. Your ability to focus on the situation.
2. How mentally tired you are.
3. How interested you are in the other person.
4. How interested you are in what is being discussed.
5. What distractions are occurring around you.

6. Where does your processing start? Some things you process start first in the conscious part of your brain. Some of your communication actions have to first be consciously and deliberately enacted. For example, when you first learned to ride a bike it may have seemed like there were too many things to remember. As you practiced it got easier because you didn't have to remember everything. Some of the easiest actions like getting on the bike, sitting on the seat, and grabbing the handlebars receded into your unconscious ready to be used when your conscious mind needed them.

The hardest actions like balance stayed in your consciousness for longer because you needed that information. (Everyone has trouble balancing a bike when they start!) After a while, you may not have even thought about anything you first learned. You just rode your bike and enjoyed the scenery. It became automatic. And it was fun!

7. How consciousness and unconsciousness "fight each other": It seems that your conscious and unconscious processes work together quite well in most situations. Sometimes, they don't however. They often "fight" each other for control (Taylor, 2022). In other words, our unconscious and conscious minds are in a constant battle for control over all aspects of our functioning. This can be a problem because in some conversations our conscious and unconscious can provide contradictory instructions.

"Fighting" may **not** be the best term for this relationship between consciousness and unconsciousness because you're using them both to help you make sense of conversations. Given the large amount of things happening around you, you need both the conscious and unconscious to help you manage everything.

8. We're not "out of control": Some research concludes that the unconscious is something we can't control. But, in reality, unconscious processes are more controlled than you may think. We're apparently aware of much unconscious communication although we don't need to pay active attention to it. Logan and Cowan (1984) believe that the automatic processes of our unconscious are actually highly controlled, intentional, and stoppable. Further, according to Logan and Cowan:

> Even when we experience "thinking" errors, such as putting the milk away in the kitchen cabinet instead of the refrigerator, this type of error "reflects fairly sophisticated behavior, done properly under close control, but with something wrong or something missing. None of them reflects random, haphazard, or uncontrolled behavior.
>
> (p. 64)

Behavior on automatic pilot, in other words, can still be coherent and accurate. An individual is aware of such automatic sequences while they are occurring in a conversation, although they don't need to pay active attention to them (Norman & Shallice, 1986). When a person does make a mistake, whatever is done is still coherent and accurate although the result may not be what the person wanted. Further, as Siegel (1999) points out:

> These "out-of-awareness" processes don't appear to be in opposition to consciousness or to anything else; they create the foundation for the mind in social interactions, internal processing, and even conscious awareness itself.
>
> (p. 263)

9. Why understanding your mind is important: So why do our minds operate this way as part of the communication process? Wouldn't it be easier to have most of our communication conscious? The problem as stated earlier is that there is so much vying for our attention that we're simply not capable of taking everything in. Further, as Bargh and Chartrand (1999) point out:

> To consciously and willfully regulate one's own behavior, evaluations, decisions, and emotional states requires considerable effort and is relatively slow. Moreover, it appears to draw on a limited resource that is quickly used up, so conscious self-regulatory acts can only occur sparingly and for a short time.
>
> (p. 16)

Our minds help by enabling us to utilize the skills we've learned over many years, learn new skills, and adapt those skills to each conversation. This is essential as we attempt to understand the complexity of conversations and the unpredictability of the people with whom we talk.

When you tailor your communication through the process of common ground connections, you must mentally choose from all the communication skills you possess. You use your current communication skills you know work for you with an emphasis on common ground and connections.

You use these skills to "successfully" communicate with all the different people with whom you interact. They all have slightly different communication "styles," and all have different likes and dislikes. You'll have more in common with some of those people than others. But, in any given conversation, you must use the tremendous power of your mind to find the things you have in common in real time.

Even with people you know you can suddenly realize that maybe you don't know them as well as you thought. For example, you've worked with a young woman for over 2 years. Over that time, you think you've come to know her pretty well. You believe you have established some degree of a common ground connection with her. One day you're having lunch with her in the cafeteria which you do quite often. Out of the blue she shares that she wants to leave her husband. This is a bombshell. She gave no indication in past conversations that her marriage was in trouble.

Suddenly you must adjust to the situation. You're not really sure what to do or say, but you'd like to help in some way without telling her what to do. In this case, you already have established common ground connections with her. You believe that maybe you can build on those connections while still using your other communication skills that you know might help.

10. Capabilities of your mind: In order to create deep common ground connections with others you need to understand: (1) neuroplasticity and (2) the natural mental tendencies you typically utilize in conversations.

(1) Neuroplasticity

Some research indicates that in normal functioning your brain forms connections and pathways that help you to process and understand everything that's going on around you. Your brain is constantly creating new connections between the neurons of your brain. When you learn something, you create new connections. This ability of your brain to literally rewire itself and change how your brain's circuits are wired is called neuroplasticity. Neuroplasticity helps you learn new things, enhance your cognitive abilities, and adapt to new situations (Kaczmarek, 2020).

But not only is neuroplasticity a positive natural trait that we all possess but you can actively use this process to improve your communication. For example, even in the act of putting forth the effort to simply pay close attention, you recalibrate your brain (Schwartz & Begley, 2002) and with astonishing speed (Ramachandran & Blakeslee, 1998).

In order to establish common ground connections, you need to tap into this natural ability of your mind to adapt to new situations. Conversations are all unique. Neuroplasticity enables you to stay flexible and adapt to the uniqueness of every conversation and person with whom you communicate.

(2) Natural mental advantages we all have in conversations.

- **Wired to connect**

  Researchers who study the human mind believe that human beings are wired to connect (Lieberman, 2013; Sukel, 2019). Suttie (2013) believes that our minds enable us to "figure out" people. Our minds allow us to bring different people together as one and get things done that we aren't able to do alone (Sukel, 2019). When you seek common ground connections, you're tapping into this "wired to connect" innate ability.

Social media use demonstrates our strong desire to connect with others. Nearly, 60% or 4.6 billion people in the world now use some form of social media. As might be expected, social media increased dramatically in the heart of the COVID-19 pandemic because of this desire to stay connected (Lee et al., 2022).

When people communicate, they obviously impact how the other person sees the world. The brain activity of one person is impacted by the brain activity of the other person. The people involved share similar thoughts and feelings. As this happens, the two brains become more in "sync." Research has shown that the brain patterns of the speaker and the listener show coordinated patterns of activity. In essence, this "wired to connect" phenomenon occurs to a certain extent in every conversation. This is understandable since every person has an innate need to connect with others (Platt & Falk, 2018).

- **Emotional contagion**

  Emotional contagion is defined as the mirroring or copying of the feelings of others. According to Gaines (2021), emotional contagion occurs when someone's emotions and behaviors lead to the same or similar emotions and behaviors in others. This is an innate capacity each of us possesses. For example, our natural reaction when someone laughs is to laugh also. Laughter is "contagious."

  You use emotional contagion in a conversation when you "sense" the feelings and emotions of others. For example, your wife is telling you about an argument she had with her boss. She's angry and wants to find another job. As she talks, you begin to feel her anger. You don't feel exactly the same emotions, but you begin in a sense to feel what she's feeling.

  This tendency we all have to "pick up" on the emotions of others isn't just with people we know well either. We can pick up the emotions of people we've just meant as well. It's hardwired into our thinking and feelings. It's even possible to demonstrate emotional contagion with someone with whom we don't have direct contact. For example, have you ever been watching television and seen someone cut themselves? You might wince along with the person in the show who cut themselves.

  Emotional contagion is a skill that each of us uses to understand and relate to others. You don't have to develop it. You already have it. The only thing you have to do is to be more aware of your natural ability and then utilize it to help you create common ground connections with others.

- **Chameleon effect**

  The chameleon effect is the unconscious equivalent of emotional contagion. With the chameleon effect, you unconsciously "catch" the feelings of others. We unintentionally mirror the nonverbal and sometimes the verbal communication of people with whom we have conversations.

You may have noticed a friend or loved one using your favorite catch-phrase or hand gestures. This is the chameleon effect. It's completely normal. In research settings, this effect has been clearly observed. If one subject in a conversation leaned back, the other person would lean back as well. If one person crossed their arms, the other person would cross his/her arms too. Later when asked neither one even realized they had mirrored the other person.

Although this effect doesn't always occur, it does happen. The chameleon effect can influence people's attitudes about their conversational partners—even their virtual partners. It generally results in more positive feelings toward the person doing the mirroring (Casasanto et al., 2020).

So why not deliberately and consciously seek to use the chameleon effect to bond with another person? If the other person crosses their arms, cross your arms too. If they move closer to you, move closer to them.

Not so fast according to research. If the other person believes you're deliberately copying what they're saying or doing, you may come off as insincere. If you're "caught" deliberately mimicking your conversational partner, you may be seen as condescending. If you try to deliberately use this chameleon effect in a manipulative way, you aren't being honest and will likely be unsuccessful. People won't like how you're communicating. You won't be able to create common ground connections either because you're violating a basic tenet of this approach which is to be honest. In fact, this may result in the opposite of the desired effect you wished to achieve. When trying to connect with others, in other words, the chameleon effect is not always positive (Liu et al., 2011; Stel et al., 2010).

The chameleon effect is tough to use as a "tool" since so much of it is out-of-awareness. Fortunately, this effect usually accompanies emotional contagion. Emotional contagion and the chameleon effect are important parts of empathy discussed further in the chapter on listening.

11. Conscious and unconscious tools: In addition to neuroplasticity and your natural mental tendencies you typically use in conversations, there are also "tools" which you can use to communicate with understanding.

Tools that start primarily in your consciousness:

(1) Your conscious observer

Your conscious observer is the running conversation in your head that goes on continually. This occurs when you're talking with someone, listening to them, observing what they're doing and still thinking and processing what's going on in the conversation. You are able to do this because you switch back and forth from one communication activity to another instantaneously. For example, you might be listening to Anita while also observing her nonverbal behaviors and the fact that there are a lot of people walking by both of you. You use all that information to adapt and modify your communication as needed.

Because your mind has a tremendous capacity and is able to change gears in a heartbeat, the conscious observer is one of your best skills in adapting your communication. It's one of the main tools in being adaptable enough to create common ground connections.

(2) Cognitive flexibility

Cognitive flexibility refers to your mind's ability to adapt to new or changing communication situations. It also refers to your ability to switch from one way of thinking to another (Miller, 2021).

Each person has a conscious ability to be "cognitively flexible." You can "choose" to be cognitively flexible or not. When you keep an open mind even though you don't agree with your conversational partner, you're being cognitively flexible. When you change your communication behaviors in a conversation to help the other person understand you, you're being cognitively flexible. When you rigidly hold on to your opinions without considering there may be other perspectives, you're *not* being cognitively flexible.

Martin and Anderson (1998) provide a good working definition of cognitive flexibility. They believe that cognitive flexibility is a person's: "(a) awareness that in any given situation there are options and alternatives available, (b) willingness to be flexible and adapt to the situation, and (c) self-efficacy or belief that one has the ability to be flexible" (p. 1).

Being cognitively flexible results in a communicator who has confidence in his/her ability to respond effectively even in new and unfamiliar situations. This means that you avoid using the same set of communication behaviors in all of your conversations. "One size" doesn't fit all.

To be cognitively flexible requires that you view what the other person is saying with as little bias or prejudice as possible. For example, you're talking to someone and they tell what you hear as a racist joke. This so offends you that you stop listening to them. You're too busy formulating a retaliatory response that will show them the error of their ways. When you're cognitively flexible, you don't quit listening. You continue to gather information on their perspective by listening even more intently.

As the conversation progresses, you may still vehemently disagree with someone, but you'll have a more accurate understanding of their point of view. For example, maybe you misunderstood them. And selfishly by completely understanding what they're saying you'll be in a better position to refute their statements and beliefs.

You're naturally cognitively flexible with different people with whom you communicate too. If you have a 3-year-old toddler, you talk with them differently than you would an adult. You think about the ways you can communicate that will help the toddler understand you. For example, maybe you get down to their level to talk with them face-to-face, use simpler words, or slow down your rate of speaking. This requires that you get in the right frame of mind in order to be cognitively flexible (Miller, 2021).

(3) Brain-to-brain links

We often don't think about the ability all of us have to mentally link up with another person in a conversation. Have you ever been in a conversation and realized that you're thinking virtually the same way as the other person? When you do this, you are in essence linking up with their mind. You and the other person are linking up "brain-to-brain." This isn't literal, but it's real.

According to Hasson (2016), our brains show similar activity or become "aligned" when we hear the same idea or story. In brain scans, Hasson found similar ideas look the same in the brain of two separate people. Further, during a conversation, the listener's brain responses are often coupled with the speaker's brain responses. Thus, we can share memories, knowledge, experiences, or anything else. Effective and meaningful communication is really a single act performed by two brains which have become in a sense "linked."

Brain-to-brain linking is a product of common ground connections. When you create common ground connections, you're really sharing a mental space with another person (Todorova, 2017). Hassan et al. (2012) label this "interpersonal space." Your ultimate goal is to share this "interpersonal space" with another human being.

You may have experienced this brain-to-brain phenomenon when talking with a good friend. In a conversation with them, you're likely to be relaxed and comfortable. There's no mental stress. You share understanding. You're on the same "wavelength." You may not think much about it since you've talked with this person so many times before, but you're again linking brain-to-brain.

When you feel this brain-to-brain connection, it's okay to openly bring this up to the other person. There's nothing wrong with checking the accuracy of your feelings. They probably had the same feelings but didn't bring them up for one reason or another. Even if you're wrong it's a compliment to the other person because it shows that you're intently listening to them and feeling a mutual connection.

How did we learn to "hook up" with others brain-to-brain? Just like the development of your communication behaviors, you've developed these brain-to-brain skills through years of talking to people and the natural abilities of your mind. You've always had this ability. It's built into the wiring of your brain. In essence, this brain-to-brain communication is common ground connections at its best.

Tools that start primarily in your unconscious

(1) Intuition

Ever had a feeling during a conversation that the other person isn't telling you the whole story? You sense they're holding something back but you don't know why you believe that. Those feelings you're having are intuitions. Your intuitions are unconscious mental processes the results of which become conscious at some point. Because your brain is constantly processing and storing information, it's also constantly comparing current experiences to past experiences. These comparisons are what create your intuitions.

You have intuitions or what are sometimes called "gut feelings" in conversations all the time. They come on all of a sudden to your conscious mind. You don't know why you're having the intuition, but you are. You often don't know what to do with these thoughts (Cholle, 2018).

The question is: Should you trust your intuitions? Sometimes you'll find them to be accurate. Sometimes not. Intuitions aren't completely understood.

For example, a woman is talking to her husband about his business trip to Houston. She gets the sense that he's not telling her the whole truth. He doesn't look at her. He keeps his space from her. Verbally he's not saying much. These verbal and nonverbal behaviors don't necessarily mean he's lying, but she has a feeling that he is. Maybe it's because he isn't communicating the way he usually does. Maybe it's because they've been having marital problems lately. It's difficult for the woman to know for sure. The woman is going through her mind searching for her stored knowledge to verify her intuitions.

Or consider another example. You're talking to a friend who's been going through a divorce. You know that she's been having a rough time. But you get the sense that she isn't being completely open about what's been going on between her and her husband. Once again you're not sure, but you have a feeling that she's not sharing everything with you. Maybe it's because you know they've been having marital problems for some time. Maybe you realize that she never discloses much about her personal life. You assume that it might just be too painful to share more than she is.

Intuitions are another example of how your conscious and unconscious processes work together to help you understand others. Intuitions are not always accurate, but they do represent another source of information in trying to understand another person. In order to create common ground connections, you need all the information you can collect from every conversation. Intuitions are another tool that you can utilize to understand and get close to people.

(2) Random thoughts

Have you ever had a thought just "pop" into your head? You remember a friend from high school. You think of the dog you had growing up. It could be anything. Everyone has these thoughts. We really don't know why this happens, but we know it does. Our minds operate sometimes with a purpose and sometimes randomly. Because your brain never rests, the possibility of random thoughts is always present.

What's important about this phenomenon is that often these "random" thoughts can be significant. Maybe a thought is reminding you of something you need to do for someone. Maybe you've been unsure about what to do with an aging parent, and you suddenly have a really good idea about a retirement home in the area. Maybe you forget to take your medication which is vital to your heart condition.

In other words, random thoughts may not be all that "random." The challenge is to determine what your random thoughts are trying to tell you. Maybe it's nothing but "a thought." It could be telling you something significant, however. The best way to determine that is if the random thought is creating strong emotion. At a minimum, random thoughts are worth exploring.

(3) Habits

Something that isn't really a tool as much as it is a way of coping is your natural tendency to form habits. Habits can help us navigate life and make our lives and communication easier, but sometimes they hold us back.

Habits are so ingrained in your unconscious that they are practically intuitive. They allow you to do things almost automatically, without any effort. For example, you may have learned that interrupting someone when they're talking is rude. You decide to always follow this no-interruption rule in your conversations. Most of the time, you don't think about it. You focus instead on other aspects of the conversation. You move this guideline into your unconscious. That doesn't mean that you never interrupt someone. It's more likely that you "catch" yourself interrupting and stop what you're doing.

Do you have other bad habits when communicating? Do you tend to talk too much? Do you always bring the topic of the conversation back to you? You may not even be aware that you have these and other bad habits because they operate in the back of your mind. They're largely unconscious.

The problem is that these poor habits are not serving you well. They've become "automatic" in not a good way. If the people with whom you communicate don't say anything about you talking too much, for example, you may continue with this bad habit without realizing it. It may have become so ingrained that it's difficult to change.

Bad habits in communication situations prevent us from operating with enough awareness to communicate to the best of our ability. How do we know if we have bad habits? Try these suggestions:

1. **Be more aware in all your conversations.** What are you doing that's contributing to the success or lack of success of your communication with others? What reactions are you getting from others?

2. **Ask the people with whom you regularly talk to give you some honest feedback about your communication.** Such a request can often be eye-opening.

3.   **Listen closely to the verbal and observe the nonverbal commu-
     nication of others when you're in the middle of conversations.**
     A grimace or puzzled facial expression can tell you a lot about how
     you're being perceived, for example. "How" someone says something
     such as the person being sarcastic can be important too.

In order to create meaningful common ground connections with others, you
must be aware of your ability to adapt to the conversation through your brain's
neuroplasticity, and use your natural tools to adapt to the conversation. That
means keeping these mental capabilities in the forefront of your mind during
your conversations so you can use them as needed. Thinking through your communication with an understanding of these aspects will enable you to adapt your
communication to the person, the situation, and the topic being discussed. This
is at the heart of creating common ground connections.

12. The mind, stereotyping, and prejudice

As human beings, we like to make sense of the world around us. We don't like
things "up in the air." When we see or meet someone, we usually make judgments about those people. We make assumptions about who they are and what
they're like based on the information we have at the time.

Sometimes with the passage of time, we change our initial assumptions about
someone. Sometimes, those initial impressions stay with us. Initial impressions
can be remarkably resistant to change. Consider just the following mental actions
we use to try to make sense of people:

1.   **Stereotyping**
2.   **Prejudice**

1. Stereotyping

Stereotypes are rigid, generalized beliefs about a person or class of people.
When we stereotype, we infer that the person with whom we're talking has
the same characteristics as everyone in the group to which we've slotted them
(MacLeod & Bodner, 2017). This practice enables us to respond rapidly to the
present situation by comparing it to past conversations we've had with similar
people. The problem is that it may lead us to ignore unique differences between
individuals.

Stereotypes enable us to simplify our world. We can slot people into certain
groups. It's just easier. We don't have to think as much when we meet a new
person, for example.

You can see why stereotyping can limit your ability to achieve common
ground connections. By definition, common ground connections are focused on

the other person and what you and that person have in common. The process will always be unique to the people and situation involved.

2. Prejudice

Prejudice is an assumption or an opinion about someone simply based on that person's membership in a particular group. Common features of prejudice include negative feelings and a tendency to discriminate against a person and other members of their assigned group (Gould, 2021). Some of the most well-known types of prejudice include racism, sexism, ageism, homophobia, nationalism, xenophobia, and religious prejudice (Gould, 2021).

13. Cultivating conscious diversity

How can we put ourselves in the best position to establish common ground connections with everyone we meet?

1. **Awareness:** One of the first ways to do this is to understand and accept that it happens. By being aware of your own natural tendency to be biased you'll be able to catch yourself more easily "in the act" and self-correct.

2. **Unconscious biases:** Remember that involuntary prejudices are developed at an early age based on the particular people with whom we interacted. If you went to a high school for example which had no Hispanics or Blacks you may have developed an unconscious bias toward those groups. You had no experiences to enable you to get to know people in these groups. To form your opinions of these groups you may have relied on the media, your friends or your family. Maybe your parents were openly racist. These experiences might have given you a biased view of Hispanics and Blacks because you had nothing else to draw from.

3. **Focus:** Jilani (2019) believes a critical skill for building bridges between different kinds of people is to focus on the individual characteristics of people rather than the groups to which they belong. This is a main tenet of common ground connections as well. That is, focus on the person with whom you're communicating in the moment.

Establishing common ground connections really helps each of us tap into the tremendous diversity that we have in this world. Diversity is our strength, not something that holds us back. When we embrace the diversity in our world we build on the strengths of people regardless of their backgrounds. In the process, we enhance our own lives and the lives of everyone who's a citizen of this world.

14. Conclusion

If you want to create closer relationships with others and create common ground connections, you need to be aware of how your brain works through your brain's conscious and unconscious processes. Each of us has a tendency toward automated communication. We must use our minds and our mental control to fight this tendency if we want to communicate to the best of our ability. By bringing more of your communication to conscious awareness, you can determine whether you're being effective in your communication and make changes as necessary.

Unfortunately, a "mental" shutdown is going on based on the extent of conflict in the world. It seems an increasing number of people have already made up their mind. Further, they have developed a dislike for anyone who doesn't agree with them. When confronted with obvious facts that disagree with their perspective, they either don't respond or create fictional narratives and conspiracy theories to support their point of view.

Each person needs to really think about their mental processes when communicating. The common ground connections approach can help with this, but we have to work to be aware of and fully utilize our minds in doing that.

Bibliography

Bargh, J. A. (1997). The automaticity of everyday life. In R. S. Wyer, Jr. (Ed.), *Advances in social cognition, vol. 10. The automaticity of everyday life: Advances in social cognition* (Vol. 10, pp. 1–61). Lawrence Erlbaum Associates Publishers.

Bargh, J. A., & Chartrand, T. L. (1999). The unbearable automaticity of being. *American Psychologist, 54*(7), 462–479.

Beres, D. (2020, November 12). 10 hidden negative effects of social media on your brain. *The Healthy.*

Berg, B. (2018, April 10). How to use the power of the subconscious mind to succeed. *Management 3.0.*

Casasanto, D., Casasanto, L. S., Gijssels, T., & Hagoort, P. (2020, July 31). The reverse chameleon effect: Negative social consequences of anatomical mimicry. *Frontiers in Psychology.*

Cherry, K. (2020, December 9). The preconscious, conscious, and unconscious minds. *Verywell Mind.*

Cherry, K. (2022, February 18). What is neuroplasticity? *Verywell Mind.*

Choi, C. Q. (2013, October 30). Human brain may be even more powerful computer than thought. *Science News (NBC News).*

Cholle, F. P. (2018, August 31). What is intuition, and how do we use it? The intuitive compass. *Psychology Today.*

Chotiner, I. (2022, May 15). Making sense of the racist mass shooting in Buffalo. *The New Yorker.*

Crist, C. (2017, February 28). On the mind: Your brain on social media. *Paste.*

de Vries, D. A., Peter, J., de Graff, H., & Nikken, P. (2016, January). Adolescents' social network site use, peer appearance-related feedback, and body dissatisfaction: Testing a mediation model. *Journal of Youth Adolescence, 45*(1), 211–224.

Dijksterhuis, A., Bos, M. W., Nordgren, L. F., & van Baaren, R. B. (2006). On making the right choice: The deliberation-without-attention effect. *Science, 311*, 1005–1007.

Fahkry, T. (2018, March 14). This is how perception creates your reality. *Mission.org*.

Finlayson, L. (2017, August 17). 5 steps to unconscious communication in conscious times. *SOCAPDigital*.

Gaines, J. (2021, February 12). What is emotional contagion theory? (Definitions and examples). *Positive Psychology*.

Gould, W. R. (2021, January 3). What is prejudice. *Verywell Mind*.

Hassan, U., Ghanzanfar, A. A, Galantucci, B., Garrod, S., & Keysers, C. (2012, February 1). Brain-to-brain coupling: A mechanism for creating and sharing a social world. *Trends in Cognitive Sciences, 16*(2), 114–121.

Hasson, U. (2016). This is your brain on communication. *TedTalk* (Neuroscientist, Uri Hasson, Explains in his TED talk That we activate our brains in the same way when, we communicate).

Jilani, Z. (2019, August 28). How to beat stereotypes by seeing people as individuals. *Greater Good Magazine*.

Kaczmarek, B. (2020). Current views of neuroplasticity; What is new and what is old. *Acta Neuropsychologica, 18*(1), 1–14.

Killingsworth, M. A., & Gilbert, D. T. (2010, November 12). A wandering mind is an unhappy mind. *Science, 330*(6006), 932.

Lavietes, M. (2022, May 17). Biden warns of 'rising hate and violence' against LGBTQ. *NBC News*.

Lee, Y., Jeon, Y. J., Kang, S., Shin, J., II, Jung, Y.-C., & Jung, S. J. (2022, May 17). Social media use and mental health during the COVID-19 pandemic in young adults: A meta-analysis of 14 cross-sectional studies. *BMC Public Health*.

Lieberman, M. D. (2013, October 8). *Social: Why our brains are wired to connect*. Crown Publishing.

Liu, J., Vohs, K. D., & Smeesters, D. (2011). Money and mimicry: When being mimicked makes people feel threatened. *Psychological Science, 22*, 1150–1151. https://doi.org/10.1177/0956797611418348

Logan, G. D., & Cowan, W. B. (1984). On the ability to inhibit thought and action: A theory of an act of control. *Psychological Review, 91*(3), 295–327.

MacLeod, C. M., & Bodner, G. E. (2017, August 9). The production effect in memory. *Sage Journals, 26*(4). https://doi.org/10.1177/0963721417691356

Marra, G. (2021, November 11). 9 interesting facts about your unconscious mind. *Clinical Hypnotherapy*.

Martin, M. M., & Anderson, C. M. (1998). The cognitive flexibility scale: Three validity studies. *Communication Reports, 11*(1), 1–9.

Mathews, A. (2019, July 6). The closed mind. *Psychology Today*.

McLeod, S. (2008). The psychology of forgetting and why memory fails. *Simply Psychology*.

Miller, L. (2021, June 15). What is cognitive flexibility, and why does it matter. *BetterUp*.

Norman, D. A., & Shallice, T. (1986). Attention to action: Willed and automatic control of behavior. In R. J. Davidson., G. E. Schwartz, & D. E. Shapiro (Eds.), *Consciousness and self-regulation* (pp. 1–14). Plenum Press.

Pietrangelo, A. (2019, December 17). What the Baader-Meinhof phenomenon is and why you may see it again . . . and again. *Healthline*.

Platt, M., & Falk, E. (2018, July 19). Wired to connect. *Psychology Today*.

Ramachandran, V. S., & Blakeslee, S. (1998). *Phantoms in the brain: Probing the mysteries of the human mind*. William Morrow.

Ricee, S. (2021, May 26). Subconscious and unconscious: The complete comparison. *Diversity for Social Impact*.

Romig, J. (2015, September 24). Speed of speech < speed of thought. *Listen Like a Lawyer*.

Schlatter, E., & Steinback, R. (2011, February 27). 10 anti-gay myths debunked. *Southern Poverty Law Center*.

Schwartz, J. M., & Begley, S. (2002). *The mind and the brain: Neuroplasticity and the power of mental force*. Regan Books/Harper Collins Publishers.

Scott, E. (2021, March 17). The stress of constantly checking your phone. *Verywell Mind*.

Shakya, H. B., & Christakis, N. A. (2017, February 1). Association of Facebook use with compromised well-being: A longitudinal study. *American Journal of Epidemiology, 185*(3), 203–211.

Shohamy, D. (2018, November 26). Retroactive and graded prioritization of memory by reward. In C. Cantor (Ed.), *When storing memories, brain prioritizes those experiences that are most rewarding*. Learning and Memory.

Siegel, D. J. (1999). *The developing mind: How relationships and the brain interact to shape who we are*. Guilford Publications.

Sifferlin, A. (2013, January 24). Why Facebook makes you feel bad about yourself. *Time*.

Stel, M., Blascovich, J., McCall, C., Mastop, J., van Baaren, R., & Vonk, R. (2010). Mimicking disliked others: Effects of a priori liking on the mimicry-liking link. *European Journal of Social Psychology, 40*, 867–880.

Sukel, K. (2019, November 13). In sync: How humans are hard-wired for social relationships. Report from Neuroscience 2019. *Dana Foundation*.

Suttie, J. (2013, December 2). Why are we so wired to connect? *Greater Good Magazine*.

Taylor, J. (2022, February 18). Our unconscious and conscious minds do battle daily. *Psychology Today*.

Thomas, J. (2022, April 5). What is preconscious and what does it mean to me? *Better Help*.

Todorova, L. (2017, May 22). On brains and science. *Donders Wonders, Opinion Post*.

4

SHOWING EMPATHY TOWARD OTHERS

Empathy allows us to connect with others. When we demonstrate empathy for others, we are showing love and compassion toward them. We are putting forth an effort to understand their experiences, needs, and wants.

Showing empathy changes us. According to Aguilar (2018):

> Empathy can open your heart, letting in more feelings, but also soften-
> ing some of the tough experiences. As we build empathy for others, we

DOI:10.4324/9781003357049-4

understand them more and can connect with them differently, which boosts our resilience—the ability to bounce back after challenges.

(Aguilar, 2018)

Demonstrating empathy also helps us to respond appropriately to the thoughts and feelings of others. It builds relationships.

Empathy changes society too. It leads us to demonstrate greater compassion and kindness for others. This makes our personal lives, communities, and the world a more united place for everyone (Orloff, 2022).

Is empathy on the decline?

Americans believe empathy has declined over the past year (Report: Is Empathy Dead in America?, 2021). In America, societal, personal, and technological changes seem to be part of the cause of this decline in empathy.

Societal

In the United States, differences among various groups have led to people "picking sides," and to people increasing to believe that the "other side" can't be trusted (Hall & Leary, 2020). It seems that people everywhere don't believe others care except if they are in their own ideological group.

Others seem indifferent to society in general. During the coronavirus pandemic, some Americans conveyed a lack of concern when they refused to socially distance and wear face coverings, or criticized those who did. The request "if you wear a mask, I'll wear a mask" to protect one another fell on deaf ears after a while. In terms of the pandemic, personal freedom trumped empathy for others (Hall & Leary, 2020).

Personal

Much like the rest of the world, America is struggling with many issues which make life in the United States society difficult:

1. Continuing coronavirus pandemic
2. Monkeypox infections
3. Racial injustice
4. Economic issues
5. Political polarization
6. Misinformation

(Hall & Leary, 2020)

In the midst of these and other problems, people need to feel other people understand what they're going through. They want to feel empathy from others. But increasingly everyone seems to be so preoccupied with their own problems that they miss opportunities to show empathy and support.

Technology

Some are suggesting that the increasing growth of technology in every part of our lives is the main culprit of our divisiveness. Social media, for example, makes communication more frequent but often only provides "superficial" connections (Brenner, 2022). You just can't demonstrate as much empathy or concern for another person on your cell phone as you can in a face-to-face conversation.

Table of contents

1. What is empathy?
2. Types of empathy
3. Empathy and common ground connections
4. Tools for demonstrating empathy
5. Empathy versus aggressive communication
6. Unique aspects of empathy
7. Becoming overwhelmed
8. Limits to empathy—desensitization
9. Conclusion

1. What is empathy?

Some studies contend that you must "feel" the same feelings as the other person in order to show empathy toward that person. You not only emotionally understand what other people feel but you also literally start to "feel" what they're feeling (Cherry, 2022).

Other studies have found that empathy is largely the ability to "understand" the situation of the other person without necessarily having to experience the same feelings. In other words, you can show empathy by "sensing" or "imagining" other people's emotions.

2. Types of empathy

The effort to define empathy can be further detailed by examining the three types of empathy: (1) cognitive, (2) affective or emotional, and (3) compassionate (Drake, 2021).

Cognitive empathy

This type of empathy is an "understanding" of someone else's feelings. It's the ability to intellectually consider other perspectives without sensing or experiencing them yourself.

Affective or "emotional" empathy

People who have emotional empathy tend to feel another person's emotions. Although not always the case, this may also include physical sensations consistent with the emotion identified with the other person. For example, if you see some-one in great distress after losing a loved one, you feel sad yourself and could even experience chest or stomach pain while observing that emotion in the other person.

Compassionate empathy or "empathetic concern"

Compassionate empathy is a combination of cognitive and emotional empathy. You recognize and understand another person's emotions and also feel them. The difference with compassionate empathy is that you may also decide to help them.

> *Example:* Torrential rains have caused an overflow of the rivers and creeks in your area of the country. The flooding has created damage to many homes. Most of your neighbors are elderly, and will have difficulty cleaning up after the flood waters recede. You know most of your neighbors, and can only imagine what they're going through. You decide to take action going up and down the streets in your area asking people what you can do to help.

3. Empathy and common ground connections

Empathy is a natural skill that helps you create common ground connections. The following are the links between the parts of this approach and the building of empathy with others:

> *Focus on the other person:* Demonstrating empathy for the other person ena-bles you to gather basic information about another person to assist you in focusing on them. You continue to demonstrate empathy throughout a conversation in order to build on the common ground connections you've established.
>
> *Create common ground:* When you meet someone for the first time, what do you generally do? You probably ask them questions to find out more about them. You listen intently to their answers as you build your "profile" of them as a person. You demonstrate empathy as you mentally detail their answers in order to understand "who" they really are. Empathy allows you to really probe into their answers so you can pick up the subtleties of each characteristic. You might find someone who likes photography, but you don't know the extent of their interest. Do they own a photography studio, or is photography just a hobby?
>
> Common ground through empathy really demonstrates to the other per-son that you're really interested in getting to know them on more than a superficial level. You're interested in not only a basic common ground but also a more detailed and very personal common ground.

Connect with others: Empathy allows you to connect with people by coordinating and aligning their feelings and interests with your own. Using empathy allows you to understand others on an increasingly personal level.

Take advantage of your current communication skills: With the common ground connections approach, you use the existing communication skills that already work for you. One of the skills you already possess is empathy. You may naturally have excellent skills in this area which you use regularly, or you may want to develop your empathy skills further.

When we use our empathy to create common ground connections, we're establishing a very personal link with another person. We're drilling down on mutual interests, beliefs, and values to a level not often experienced in conversations. We feel close to another person. Our conversations "feel good."

4. Tools for demonstrating empathy

The following are communication "tools" that will help you to demonstrate empathy toward another person and ultimately create common ground connections. Some of these you may already utilize to a greater or lesser extent.

Tool #1: build rapport
Tool #2: work to develop interpersonal sensitivity

Tool #1: build rapport

Do you have a friend with whom you feel "comfortable"? When you talk with them it feels as if you can say anything. You don't have to plan what you want to say. It just naturally flows. You get the sense the other person feels the same way. Both of you are sensitive to not only what the person says but also the emotions behind it. There is something about how you relate to one another that works and feels better than with any other person (Huntington, 2022).

What you are experiencing with your friend is rapport. When people have rapport between them, they're focused and invested in one another. Rapport is when you "click" with another person (Tickle-Degnen & Rosenthal, 1990). You build rapport largely through your demonstration of empathy.

Tool #2: work to develop interpersonal sensitivity

Interpersonal sensitivity is the ability and motivation to read others through a focus on their verbal and nonverbal communications. It involves seeking to understand someone's state of mind by being attentive, trusting your intuitions, and demonstrating empathy (Sabater, 2022). To be sensitive to others you must be open to perceiving and responding effectively to the emotions of others.

Some people have more sensitivity than others, but sensitivity is a quality of thinking and relating on which you can work. You can choose to be more or less sensitive to another person.

If you're motivated to work on your sensitivity, you first must be open to perceiving and responding to others. Learn from your interactions as you develop your skills. Allow yourself to be influenced and affected by others.

5. Empathy versus aggressive communication

When you experience "aggressive" communication by the person with whom you're having a conversation, it doesn't feel good. Aggressive communication occurs when the person tries to control and/or take over a conversation. It's more important for the other person to direct the show and talk about what they want to talk about than it is to listen to you.

Aggressive communication is really the opposite of common ground connections. Aggressive communicators aren't trying to link up or understand the other person. A person who is aggressive is really only interested in sharing their own perspective. They're not listening much to you. They're not showing empathy toward you. Consider the following aggressive conversational actions.

Offering advice without being asked

When your partner does this, they're really telling you how to "fix" yourself. This shows impatience on their part that is an outgrowth of not wanting to really take the time to listen fully to your problem.

Only offer advice if the other person asks. They may not want to hear your solutions anyway. They probably just want someone to listen and empathize with them.

Constantly interrupting you to provide a solution or to share their views on a situation

Interrupting someone is really saying "I want to share my thoughts which I think are more important than yours." It demonstrates to the other person that you're not listening. If you were listening for example, you might respond to what the other person had just said.

Talking more than you listen

If someone talks non-stop or without even considering bringing you into the conversation, they're being aggressive. They're going to talk to the point you'll quit trying to really contribute anything. People tire of having to work too hard to break in to a conversation just to say something. Often these aggressive people win because it's just not worth the effort to do battle with someone "for the floor."

Failing to adjust to the other person's speaking and listening style

If you really want to show empathy, you have to be willing to adjust your style to the person with whom you're talking. For example let's say the person with whom you're talking is more introspective, thoughtful, and sometimes has trouble expressing his/her opinions. Being able to adapt to this style of communication is a basic tenet of empathy and ultimately of establishing common ground connections. In this case you may be amazed at what you find out about that person just by showing empathy.

6. Unique aspects of empathy

There are some parts of empathy that are unlike any other aspects of communication. The two most common are (1) empathic accuracy and (2) effort versus effectiveness.

Empathic accuracy

Empathic accuracy means the extent to which you're able through your use of empathy to successfully infer the specifics of another person's thoughts and feelings. When you work to accurately read the other person, they appreciate your efforts. The relationship is strengthened.

Keep in mind that being completely honest and accurate through your empathy can sometimes be negative. Consider the following instances when sharing the information you've gathered from your empathic accuracy may not be the best idea:

- **Misperceptions of your partner:** For example, do you evaluate and share all the actions of your partner and do so in a negative light? Demonstrating empathy does not involve evaluation of others.
- **Unpleasant truths:** One partner's empathic accuracy may be painful for both people in the relationship. There are times when insights that might be painful for the other person are best not shared. Perhaps the issue can be brought up in a less painful way in order to successfully resolve it.
- **Irreconcilable differences:** There may be times when the relationship is not going to survive for a number of reasons. Using your empathic accuracy to point out obvious differences that are really irreconcilable, probably won't help.

Empathic accuracy can lead to insights that will contribute to the long-term health of a relationship. But it also points to the importance of being aware that you don't always have to share what you pick up. Be sensitive to how the other person feels and what impact the information will have on that person, not how good you are at "reading" the other person.

Effort versus effectiveness

Empathy is unlike most other communication concepts in that you don't have to be good at it to have a positive effect on people. Generally, people are more interested in the fact you tried to show empathy toward them. In other words, it's more important to the other person that you attempted to understand their issue than it is to be accurate about what those issues are. Relatively unsophisticated strategies might do the best job of comforting another in a specific situation. You can't be "wrong" only absent in your efforts.

7. Becoming overwhelmed

Each of us can sometimes feel overwhelmed trying to empathize with others. This situation can lead us to experience the following: (1) empathic distress and (2) empathic fatigue.

Empathic distress

When we observe suffering in the world, we sometimes want to ignore or withdraw from exposing ourselves to any more information about that situation (Singer & Klimecki, 2014). When news of a disaster somewhere in the country is shown on the news, you might switch the station.

This can happen on a personal level as well. If I'm a health-care worker in a nursing home, I may get to the point that I'm finding it increasingly difficult to help people anymore. I get more and more distressed by the hopelessness of the people in my care. The distress is greater than my capacity for continuing to demonstrate empathy.

Empathic fatigue

If you're distressed for long enough, eventually empathy "fatigue" sets in. You end up exhausting what you can give to others. Your ability to relate to and care for others through empathy is not an unlimited resource. If you don't pull back to get some perspective and recharge, you can end up with first, empathy distress and then empathy fatigue. We often aren't even aware that we're becoming fatigued in this way despite our mental and physical symptoms (Goecker, 2019).

When we become overwhelmed by the requirements of empathy required in our life, the question becomes: "How can I support others through empathy without 'losing myself' in the process?" Understanding empathic distress and empathic fatigue may assist you in helping others through your empathy without hurting yourself in the process.

8. Limits to empathy—desensitization

When people experience empathic distress and empathic fatigue for long enough, they can become "numb" or "desensitized." That is, they begin to feel less shock and distress by scenes of human distress because of overexposure to such scenes (Slovic, 2007).

Psychic numbing

It's hard to grasp the enormity of many crises when we're not personally involved with them. As of July 2022, over a million people in the United States had died from the coronavirus disease. 6.4 million people had died worldwide (Elflein, 2022). Each death is a tragedy to that person's friends and family but may not be felt as much by others who don't know the person. If someone gets the coronavirus or knows someone who does, it has more impact. It personalizes it.

But it's hard to grasp the numbers when they're in the millions (Wen, 2020). This is called psychic numbing. As the numbers of deaths increase our feelings often don't commensurately increase as well. It's all too much to contemplate. I protect my sanity by becoming numb to the whole thing.

For example, as of August 2022, more than 114,000 new COVID-19 infections were reported every day in the United States. Infection rates in many states continue to rise. The mortality rate, which had declined, rose again, amounting to more than 350 deaths per day. In total, more than 1 million people in the United States have died from the coronavirus pandemic as of August 2022 (The Covid-19 Global Pandemic, 2022).

How can we wrap our minds around such numbers? We may become desensitized because the numbers of people suffering and dying continue to grow beyond our ability to cope. How does this desensitization happen? The factors include the following: (1) experiences become less and less personal, (2) what can I personally do?, (3) I don't have the skills, and (4) there's no obvious reward.

Experiences become less and less personal

We might be able to understand the experiences of one or two people particularly if we know them. But as the numbers of people struggling increase, the data mean less and less to us personally. The suffering doesn't impact us in our day-to-day lives (Slovic, 2007) so we may not even think about it.

What can I personally do?

The problem may seem so large that you alone may not feel you can have an impact. My donation to the appropriate charity, for example, may feel like a drop in the bucket so why contribute at all?

I don't have the skills

People often avoid showing empathy because they feel they're not good at it in particular situations (Goecker, 2019). If I feel I don't have the necessary skills, I might even make things worse.

There's no obvious reward

There's often no reward for showing empathy toward others. Sometimes, when we try to express empathy, instead of compassion and understanding, we get anger or judgment expressed toward us. Some people don't want your empathy.

9. Conclusion

In difficult times, where do we start to heal the divisiveness in the United States and the world? One way is to start by using common ground connections to increase the empathy we show to one another.

Focus on the other person

In order to really empathize with someone, we have to understand them and what problems they're experiencing. Only by focusing on that person through empathy can we get the information we need from them to eventually create common ground connections.

Find common ground

In order to create common ground connections, we first have to establish common ground. We need to identify common interests that we share with someone. We continue to use our empathy skills to learn the information we need from them. Focusing on commonalities can lead to a deeper understanding of another person. Be curious about the other person's experiences. Learn more about what has happened to them and how they felt.

Connect don't avoid

Once you've established common ground on a number of issues, you then empathize with that person to go deeper to establish a connection on some of those issues. We can't be afraid to try to connect with people who hold opinions different from our own. When we avoid those conversations, we don't change anything. We just perpetuate divisiveness.

We're changed

As we increase our use of empathy in our conversations with others, we're changed. We begin to understand and even "feel" what others are experiencing. Our world expands to include others and all that they experience. The depth and frequency of the common ground connections in our lives increases. We understand that ultimately we are not alone in dealing with life's tough experiences.

Bibliography

Aguilar, E. (2018, February 6). The power of empathy. *Edutopia*.

Brenner, M. (2022). Why we are facing an empathy deficit. *Thrive Global*.

Cherry, K. (2022, July 21). What is empathy? *Verywell Mind*.

Cromwell, H. (2021, June 25). America's empathy problem—and what to do about it. *The Baltimore Sun*.

Despart, Z. (2022, July 17). "Systemic failures" in Uvalde shooting went far beyond local police, Texas House report details. *The Texas Tribune*.

Dixon-Fyle, S., Dolan, K., Hunt, D. V., & Prince, S. (2020, May 19). Report: Diversity wins: How inclusion matters. *McKinsey and Company*.

Drake, K. (2021, July 21). Is it possible to lack empathy? *PsychCentral*.

Duffy, B., & Gottfried, G. (2018). *BBC global survey: A world divided*. Ipsos MORI Social Research Institute.

Elflein, J. (2022, July 27). Total number of U.S. coronavirus (COVID-19) cases and deaths July 22, 2022. *Statista*.

Goecker, L. (2019, May 9). Are we becoming less empathic by choice? *The Swaddle*.

Hall, J., & Leary, M. (2020, September 17). The U.S. has an empathy deficit. *Scientific American*.

Huntington, C. (2022). *Rapport: Definition & how to build it*. Berkeley Well-Being Institute.

Indeed Editorial Team. (2021, September 8). 20 ways to build rapport. *Indeed*.

Jimenez, J. (2021, July 16). Compassion vs. empathy: Understanding the difference. *Better Up*.

Krull, E. (2022, April 28). Sympathy, empathy, and compassion: What's the difference? *Cake*.

Lardieri, A. (2018, April 25). Survey: Majority of people around the world feel divided. People around the world feel more divided today than they did 10 years ago. *U.S. News and World Report*.

Leach, M. J. (2005, November). Rapport: A key to treatment success. *Complement Therapy Clinical Practice*, *11*(4), 262–265.

Manning, K. (2021, July 26). The role of small connections in inclusion. *Psych Central*.

Morin, A. (2022). The importance of showing empathy to kids who learn and think differently. *Understood*.

Palmer, B. (2020, March 2). What science tells us about overcoming divisiveness. *The National Interest*.

Report: Is Empathy Dead in America? (2021, October 27). Method communications. *Cision, PR Newswire*.

Sabater, V. (2022, July 28). Interpersonal sensitivity: The key to understanding others. *Exploring Yourmind*.

Simon-Thomas, E. (2020, February 11). Find social media frustrating? Try empathy. *University of California, Berkeley's Greater Good Science Center, UC Newsroom*.

Singer, T., & Klimecki, O. M. (2014, September 22). Empathy and compassion. *Current Biology*, *24*(18), R875–R878.

Slovic, P. (2007). *Psychic numbing and genocide*. American Psychological Association.

Statista Research Department. (2022, July 5). People shot to death by U.S. police 2017–2022, by race. *Statista*.

Tickle-Degnen, L., & Rosenthal, R. (1990). The nature of rapport and its nonverbal correlates. *Psychological Inquiry*, *1*(4), 285–293.

Washington, E., & Patrick, C. (2018, September 17). 3 requirements for a diverse and inclusive culture. *Gallup Workplace*.

Wen, T. (2020, June 30). What makes people stop caring? *BBC*.

5

TARGETED SPEAKING AND NONVERBAL PINPOINTING

Targeted speaking

When you target your speaking, you adjust your language throughout each conversation to make sure the other person can understand what you're sharing. You use this skill all the time in a typical conversation. Labeling it "targeted" speaking is merely calling your attention to the fact that it's a good idea, and that you might want to try to use it more often.

DOI:10.4324/9781003357049-5

Nonverbal pinpointing

In order to be successful in getting the information needed to create common ground connections, you need to tune into what can be a largely **untapped** source of information—nonverbal communication. Untapped because you tend to focus on what people say, not what they do. And yet most of the meaning in a conversation is carried in the nonverbal channel.

This section of the chapter introduces a new concept in understanding the nonverbal communication of others called nonverbal pinpointing. Nonverbal pinpointing is learning to identify specific nonverbal behaviors that will give you the best chance of understanding the other person in the present conversation. You consciously choose which nonverbal information to process and what to ignore.

Targeted speaking and nonverbal pinpointing

As humans we seek to be in relationship with others. We need each other (Sreenivasan & Weinberger, 2016). Relationships are important to both our physical and mental well-being. People with less social interactions and relationships tend to have poor immunity and a greater chance of heart disease and cancer (DiGiulio, January 9, 2018). Social isolation and loneliness can even be risk factors for increased chances of death (Holt-Lunstad et al., 2015).

One of the main ways you form and maintain your relationships is through your verbal and nonverbal communications. We often don't think about our skills in these areas. We communicate like we always have. In essence, you take your ability to communicate verbally and nonverbally for granted. You've developed and used your skill set since before you can remember. You've learned the verbal and nonverbal skills that work for you in most situations. You naturally use those skills in the majority of your conversations. And generally those skills work.

But what happens when they don't? Everyone has conflicts and disagreements with others. In these instances, each of us tries to figure out what went wrong. Our default is often: "It can't be me." Or we write off the conflict as a one-time event as in: "Jerry must be having a rough day. I really enjoy talking with him most of the time." The truth is that sometimes the problem is "us."

Common ground connections and verbal/nonverbal communication

How you communicate verbally and nonverbally is obviously important in your efforts to create common ground connections. This can be demonstrated in the following ways.

Focus on the other person

In order to establish common ground connections, you must focus on the other person. One of the best ways to do that is to understand the other person's verbal and nonverbal communications. Because there are so many ways that information can be interpreted, this can be a challenge. Words can have multiple meanings or not be understood at all, and the range of nonverbal behaviors and their meanings can vary widely from person to person.

Establish common ground

Your verbal and nonverbal communications give you the information you need to identify common ground with the other person. That common ground means that both people must use language and complementary nonverbal behaviors that the other person understands. Both must monitor the conversation to make sure that happens.

Connect with others

As you create a connection with the other person, you begin to use verbal and nonverbal communication behaviors that are increasingly similar. You "in a sense" are building communication that is unique to you and the other person with whom you're having a conversation. You may have experienced this yourself with someone with whom you're close now. You and your brother, for example, may have developed certain words and language that both of you understand but would be unknown to others.

Be flexible in communicating

When you establish common ground connections, you begin to understand the uniqueness of the other person's verbal and nonverbal communications. You learn to adapt to that person's unique skill set as you learn what it takes to connect with them. In the same way, you are flexible in your communication so that you can communicate in such a way that the other person understands.

Take advantage of your current communication skills

You already have a set of verbal and nonverbal communication skills that work for you now. Continue to use those skills but also be willing to adapt to the current conversation.

Preview of chapter

This chapter asks you to critically examine your current verbal and nonverbal communication skills. You'll soon realize those instances when you're really good at your communication, and those situations where you might want to improve. The chapter sections are as follows:

1. Verbal/nonverbal communication in the world
2. Individual verbal/nonverbal communication

1. Verbal/nonverbal communication in the world

The verbal and nonverbal communications we currently use in the United States not only can bring people together but also can create and perpetuate differences. Consider just two examples of how these channels of communication can isolate people from one another, create conflict, and can sometimes even stir violence: (1) labeling and (2) using symbols.

Verbal communication—example: labeling

One way we verbally perpetuate differences is by labeling individuals and groups, such as using a word or short phrase to identify and describe a person according to age, sex, national origin, education, and other characteristics. Labeling helps us slot people into neat categories. It's just easier to label someone and then interact with them based on that label. Unfortunately, the label we give to others might not be accurate.

As this practice has increased in the United States, separation from one another and unconscious prejudice have increased. People can label you lazy because you're overweight. You can be labeled as gorgeous because you're physically beautiful. People who think you're promiscuous will label you a slut (Tollshein, 2019).

Factors like class and race can be important in how groups are labeled. For example, actions like skipping school and stealing fruit from people's trees are often considered typical juvenile behaviors. In poorer areas, however, similar conduct is often considered juvenile delinquency (Crossman, 2020).

The problem is that people are much more than any label someone can put on them (Haltiwanger, 2014). Because labels skew how we perceive people, they can promote conscious and unconscious prejudices. And ultimately we limit our ability to really know them. Further, our communication isn't on target.

The practice of labeling other people is not only increasing but also becoming more negative and disparaging in the process. Labels like White Nationalist, Nazis, right, left, Fundamentalist, and all kinds of other words and phrases are used to slot people into negative categories. We then interact with those people based on the label we assign them not on who they really are. Once someone is labeled that label tends to stick in the minds of others too.

Labeling someone doesn't provide you with much flexibility in trying to understand them. Each person is unique and can change from one day to the next. You may understand this yourself. Do you communicate exactly the way you did 5 years ago? Do you communicate the same way with someone today that you did when you first met them? Probably not.

Nonverbal communication—example: symbols

We also perpetuate divisions in the country through our nonverbal communication. An example is the nonverbal symbols we use. Nonverbal symbols are defined as visual objects or references used to identify a person, place, or thing. For example, many groups have symbols and flags which members rally around and which strengthen the cohesiveness in these groups. It helps them rally around a cause with other like-minded people. Symbols can include numbers, hate group logos, acronyms (KKK), flags, and overt physical actions like a white power fist raised at a rally (Stroud, August 29, 2018).

A number of different flags were symbols on January 6, 2021, representing the many diverse groups demonstrating at the United States Capitol. The stars and bars of the Confederate flag, the original Nazi party flag, and the Join or Die Flag first created by Benjamin Franklin were all on display (Romey, 2021).

Nonverbal symbols in the world

The same nonverbal sign or symbol can mean different things in countries around the world. Making a circle with your thumb and index finger indicates "okay" in the United States (Anderson et al., 2019). In other countries, however, this same "okay" sign can mean different things. In Italy, Greece, Iran, Venezuela, Brazil, Turkey, and Iraq, the "okay" sign is an insulting gesture, especially to LGBT+ people. In France, it means zero or worthless (Halcrow, 2019).

Symbols can also "morph" or change over time. In the United States, the okay gesture has now been classified as a symbol of hate by the Anti-Defamation League. White supremacy groups and the far right have started including the "okay" gesture in their demonstrations as identifiers of their groups (Allyn, 2019).

Verbal labeling and nonverbal symbols

How we use our verbal and nonverbal communications is sometimes the cause of problems but can also be the solution in relating to others. It's at the core of creating common ground connections which are so important at this time when our basic communication needs to bring people together.

2. Individual verbal/nonverbal communication

Verbal versus nonverbal communication

In a general sense, you use verbal communication to help you categorize and comprehend the content of what the other person says. Nonverbal communication can't really do that. Nonverbal behaviors communicate your emotions or how you feel about the information you're communicating or understanding from others (Cherry, 2021).

A simplified way of looking at this is that verbal communicates content. Nonverbal communicates emotion. But it's often not that simple. Verbal and nonverbal behaviors are usually inextricably intertwined. But, sometimes the verbal and nonverbal communication of the other person can be contradictory. For example you might realize that a person is smiling at you while at the same time saying something insulting.

Nonverbal and verbal communications also differ in "how" information is communicated. With verbal communication you talk, stop, listen, and then may talk further. There is a definite beginning and end. With nonverbal communication, however, your communication never stops. You're constantly communicating with your nonverbal behaviors whether you intend to or not. Just standing in one place without moving is still communicating something.

Also, because of the continuous nature of nonverbal behaviors, there is just more information available than with verbal communication. Some estimates are that often as much as 90% of the meaning in a conversation is carried through the nonverbal channel. Admittedly, because of the many aspects of nonverbal communication, the information is more complex, but it's still there if you take advantage of it. Verbal communication is limited because in most instances you don't talk non-stop. If you do, people may become bored, irritated, or start ignoring you (Carlson, 2022).

3. Paralanguage

Helping you understand the meaning of the verbal and nonverbal communications of others is a concept called "paralanguage." You might think of paralanguage as communication that's "between" verbal and nonverbal communications. It includes "how" you say something like accent, pitch, volume, speech rate, modulation, and fluency. If you "sigh" after someone says something, they might think you disagree or are bored. But the other person won't know for sure (Nordquist, 2019). Identifying the differences between paralanguage, verbal communication and nonverbal communication is not always easy in a typical conversation (Matthews, 2014).

Sometimes that identification is easier than at other times. Let's say you ask someone to go to the store with you. They say: "Yeah, I'd love to go to the grocery with you," but say it sarcastically. In this case, you probably believe the sarcastic paralanguage rather than what the person actually said verbally. You realize you're going to the store alone.

At other times, understanding what the other person is talking about is nearly impossible. For example, in talking with your wife you know she's heartbroken over her mother's recent death. She tells you: "Oh, I'm fine. I know she was almost a hundred." She's saying she's fine, but you get the feeling she isn't. When she says she's fine, she's also speaking quietly, and saying it in a really depressed, non-emotional way. Reading the aspects of your wife's paralanguage will help you get to her true feelings and hopefully be able to help.

Paralanguage helps you identify even nuanced meaning being communicated by others. It can help you zero in on what the person is really communicating. It thus makes your common ground connections more accurate.

4. Verbal communication basics

To humans, words are more than a means of communication. They can shape our beliefs, behaviors, feelings, and ultimately our actions. For example, we now know that our choice of words has a direct and immediate effect on our emotional response. Words make our brains inclined to respond in specific ways. This is true whether we're reacting to spoken words delivered by someone else, or to the inner self-talk we hear ourselves "saying" inside our heads.

Words can hurt. You can really tear someone up with mean words you direct at them. And we tend to take what people say literally. There's little nuance when someone says to you: "You're a jerk." Of course, we still filter what people say to us through our own filters, but some language is undeniable.

And what people hear is what counts. When it comes to language and communication, the rule is it's not what you say but what people hear. This is why you should ask for feedback from the other person to make sure they understand what you say.

5. Word barriers—English

The complexity of words and the different meanings that can be conveyed is enormous. The English language is made up of almost a million words. An average adult can readily recall and use around 20,000 English words as well as recognize and know the meaning of approximately 20,000 more words (Kelly, 2017). The number of potential words we can use is impressive. The problem is that the real meaning of those words often varies from person to person.

Added to this complexity is the use of vague and imprecise language by nearly everyone. Do your friends describe the concert they attended the previous night as "weird?" Or if you ask a friend how a date went, and they say it was "nice." Or they call specific objects "stuff?" Or they talk about "those guys" who will be at the football game.

The problem in all these cases is that you probably don't know specifically what the other person is talking about. Who are "those guys?" What did they mean that the concert was "weird?"

Common word barriers

Word barriers are aspects of verbal communication that get in the way of mutual understanding in a conversation. They can occur not only when we "misuse" words and language but also when we misinterpret the words and language of others. Consider the following barriers:

Barrier #1: Selfish processing of word meanings. Essential to creating common ground connections is the necessity for both people in a conversation to share an understanding of the words and language being used. That means both parties need to understand whether the other person has the same meaning for the words being used.

You might be talking to your friend about a person in your community who you describe as a "3 percenter." You say, "Oh, he's a 3 percenter if you know what I mean." The problem is that your friend may never have heard of this far-right militia movement and paramilitary group. You've assumed incorrectly that your friend knows about this group. Or you say, "Betty is a real right winger when it comes to politics." The problem here is that there are many definitions of what is meant by "right winger." You'll need to define exactly what you mean by that to your friend to have an intelligent conversation.

It can work the other way too. You're talking to someone and they describe Rosa's dress and appearance as "ostentatious." You don't know what "ostentatious" means. At that point the only thing you can think about is: "I wonder what ostentatious means?" You're no longer listening or processing what the other person is saying (London, 2018). In other words be careful about assuming that the person with whom you're talking shares the same meaning for the words you're using in a conversation.

We all use a vocabulary we've developed over a period of many years. It's somewhat unique to us. We usually don't think about the words we're using. But, if we're to remove this barrier, we must stay alert for possible differences in the meaning of words and check to make sure the other person understands.

Barrier #2: Messages can range from concrete to abstract. Abstract terms refer to ideas that can't be physically described such as love or democracy. For example the term "leisure activities" is very abstract because it's so general and could include any number of different activities such as "sports," "hobbies," or "games." Concrete terms are very specific. If you describe your dog as a collie instead of just a "dog" you're being concrete.

Ideally, your communication will benefit by using more concrete words and language. When you communicate using "abstract" language you leave open too many possibilities for different interpretations by the people involved in the conversation. When you communicate in a more concrete manner, you decrease the chances that your words and language will be misunderstood. More abstract terms can often convey more imaginative meanings and thus have their place as long as the people in the conversation have a common understanding of what's being communicated.

Barrier #3: Confirming and disconfirming messages. Confirming messages take place when you acknowledge others through your communication. When your daughter brings home artwork from school, her parents can support her or not. A confirming response from the parents would be to compliment the daughter on her abilities, and put the picture on the refrigerator. A disconfirming response would be if the girl's parents ignore the child's efforts or make fun of the picture.

The idea is to create "shared" meaning in every conversation. This happens when the words used in a conversation mean the same to all participants.

6. Word barriers—International

Internationally, word and language barriers can occur when people don't share a common language. Although many people in the world speak English, that doesn't mean everyone completely understands English (Neeley, 2012). Even within the same country, regional dialects or regional varieties can make it difficult for those people to understand one another. The United Kingdom has 37 different dialects. India uses over 720 dialects (Gratis, 2022).

Different "accents" can also create communication problems. Accents are unique ways of pronouncing words of a different language based on your primary language. If the person's accent is "heavy," this can cause difficulty in understanding what is said (Gratis, 2022).

Seeking common ground connections with a person with whom you don't share a common language requires patience and respect for that person. Be willing to work with them to overcome the language barrier so both of you can understand.

7. Nonverbal communication basics

In order to be a successful in creating common ground connections, you need to tune into what can be a largely untapped source of information—nonverbal communication. Untapped because you tend to focus on what people say, not what they do. And yet most of the meaning in a conversation is carried through the nonverbal channel.

A straightforward definition of nonverbal communication is communication without words. However, nonverbal communication is more complex than this. The different types of nonverbal behaviors alone demonstrate this complexity including the face, eyes, touch, personal space, clothing, time, and even scent. Each of these is comprised of many aspects which have a broad range of meanings. Those meanings can be based on a number of factors including the context of the conversation and the closeness of the relationship (Cherry, 2021). The following concepts help explain the importance of nonverbal communication: (1) nonverbal communication is unique, (2) nonverbal communication is complex, and (3) attend to facial microexpressions.

Nonverbal communication is unique

Understanding the nonverbal communication of others means being aware of the following unique aspects of this channel of communication:

You cannot not communicate.

As indicated earlier, you are always communicating "something" nonverbally. Even if you just stand emotionless you are still communicating (Watzlawick et al., 1967).

Everyone's nonverbal behaviors are slightly unique to them.

For example you may have a friend who makes big gestures when he speaks. You don't know anyone who gestures quite like your friend. That's just how he talks. A realization of this helps you accept and understand him.

You can't read all the nonverbal behaviors of the other person.

In any given day you're exposed to thousands of nonverbal behaviors from others in your life. What this means is that you must choose what nonverbal behaviors to which you will pay attention and which you will ignore.

Your nonverbal observations aren't always correct.

What's apparent is that sometimes we're pretty good at reading the nonverbal communication of others. Sometimes we're not. And when you think about it, can you really be sure you correctly match what you observe on the "*outside*" with what's happening on the "*inside*" of another person? Plus, there are thousands of nonverbal behaviors available in any conversation. Will you always be able to pick the right ones to understand someone?

Many nonverbal signals don't have one specific meaning.

If you've ever had someone wink at you and didn't know why, you've probably experienced this uncertainty. Did they wink to express their affection for you, their pleasure with something you just did, or because they think that you and them share some inside knowledge or joke that you don't remember?

Be aware of societal generalizations.

Often you hear the interpretation that when someone crosses their arms it means they're erecting a barrier between themselves and the people with whom they're communicating. They're closing themselves off and don't want to communicate. But might crossed arms be communicating something else? Maybe the person is stretching their back and it just feels good to cross their arms. Maybe they just like to cross their arms. Maybe they're cold. Be wary of using a stereotypical interpretation of a nonverbal action, without following up with the person to make sure of the meaning.

Nonverbal communication is complex

It's ironic that the communication channel that provides us with the most information in conversations is also the channel that can confuse us the most. Nonverbal communication is so complex that it isn't always easy to accurately understand what others are communicating. For example, consider the complexity of facial expressions. We each have 52 separate facial muscles which can produce at least 27 different emotions or combinations of emotions (Cowen & Keltner, 2017).

The value in understanding nonverbal behaviors is to gather information about the other person to guide you in your conversations with them. For example, if someone appears disinterested in what you're saying, it could be a lot of things not just that they're bored. They might just be tired and would have trouble listening to anyone.

Facial microexpressions

A prime example of the complexity of nonverbal behaviors is reflected in the face and specifically facial microexpressions. Have you ever had an uneasy feeling when meeting someone: "I don't know what it is, but there's just something about that person that makes me feel uncomfortable." Or you take a look at someone, and immediately "like" them. We usually chalk this up to instinct or a "gut feeling," but researchers have found these feelings can come from what are called "microexpressions."

Microexpressions are emotions that are displayed or flashed across the whole face or one region of the face in as quickly as 1/25 of a second. They occur so fast that they're not often perceived consciously by either person in a conversation (Zetter, 2003). When we experience an emotion, our faces exhibit an expression that matches that emotion. This can often be without our knowledge. Microexpressions show exactly how someone feels, no matter how hard they try to conceal it (Van Edwards, Science of People).

Microexpressions are difficult to read because we're not experienced or trained in "how" to do that. We can increase our ability to process microexpressions by, first of all, paying particular attention to someone's face during every conversation. See if you can detect even small variations between what they're communicating and any of their facial expressions. Second, trust your intuition. If you notice what you think is a tiny facial movement on a person with whom you're interacting ask yourself: "What might that mean?" Finally, know that human beings have the innate ability to subconsciously detect microexpressions (Wezowski, 2018).

8. Nonverbal communication—International

When communicating with someone who's from a different part of the world, it's always a good idea to be aware of unique nonverbal behaviors of that person. Nonverbal behaviors can be the same or very similar, but they can also be very different from person to person across the globe. Consider how different just the practice of shaking hands across the world is.

Shaking hands

Shaking hands is a common practice in many parts of the world. In Brazil and the United States, people are expected to give a firm handshake. A French handshake is a single downward motion, firm, and brief. People in Britain offer a "lighter" handshake. Shaking hands in Asia can be considered rude. People in Thailand don't shake hands at all (The ThoughtCo Team, 2019).

In the United States, there is also what's known as the DAP handshake. This occurs when two people greeting one another bring their hands up together and grasp each other's thumb. Then they will raise this joint hand coupling up in the air and bring their respective fist to their chest. DAP stands for dignity and pride. First developed by Black soldiers during the Vietnam War, this DAP handshake indicated a unity among Black soldiers who were facing racism in their own country (Vaughn, 2020). Many Black people and others within the United States have since adopted this type of handshake.

In seeking common ground connections, we have to be aware of each person's ways of communicating nonverbally. If we try to reach broad conclusions based on "typical" nonverbal behaviors of some people, we may miss the uniqueness of the person with whom we're communicating.

9. When the verbal and nonverbal communications conflict

Whenever there is a discrepancy between someone's verbal and nonverbal communications, typically we pay more attention to the nonverbal communication. We've come to understand over our lifetime, that the nonverbal communication of others will give us not only more information but also more accurate information.

We've learned that people including ourselves can control "what" we say much more than "how" we say something. This is because your verbal behaviors are much more under our control than your nonverbal behaviors. Nonverbal behaviors can often be unconscious, and can often "leak" out without your awareness. You might be able to hide what you're really feeling through your words, but your nonverbal behaviors often give you away.

For example, if you're in a job interview, the interviewer may ask: "You seem nervous." She's not getting that impression through what you say but, what your body is communicating through shaking, sweating, and other outward signs. Or consider how you react when someone gives you what sounds like a compliment: "You look great," but doesn't say it very enthusiastically. Are you more likely to believe the verbal or the nonverbal?

The rule of thumb to use in understanding conflicting verbal and nonverbal communications is:

> **If the verbal and nonverbal communication conflict—believe the nonverbal.**

This rule of thumb doesn't mean you should ever ignore or necessarily diminish what a person says. Verbal communication always communicates something, and sometimes it communicates much more than the other person's nonverbal behaviors .

Resolving this discrepancy between the other person's verbal and nonverbal communications is important when you're trying to establish common ground connections. If you can't differentiate what information shared is true and what's not, you may believe you're establishing common ground connections when you're really not.

10. Your mind and verbal/nonverbal communication

The next section of this chapter details how your mind works when you communicate through the verbal and nonverbal channels. All these actions happen almost instantaneously and together in a conversation at an incredible speed.

Verbal—conscious and unconscious processing

Language and thinking are closely intertwined. When your mind is unclear, your language is too.

Conscious awareness is important in any communication situation but is particularly important with the words and language you use to communicate with others. This is how each of us makes sure that we're helping the other person understand us. You mentally listen to yourself when you're speaking, observe the other person's reactions to what you're saying, and pay attention to their feedback. This is how you determine whether you're being understood. If you're explaining a brand new project to a work colleague that's extremely technical, you consciously monitor whether you're getting through to them. You ask them if they understand you. If it appears that you're not or they simply say, "I'm not following you," then you adjust your instructions accordingly.

Unfortunately, we don't always think about the words and language we use. We process many of the aspects of verbal communication at an unconscious level. We verbally communicate out of habit more than anything else. When you do become aware of your language it's usually because there is an obvious misunderstanding or some problem.

Nonverbal communication—conscious and unconscious processing

Messages conveyed and received through nonverbal behaviors can occur with or without conscious awareness (DePaulo & Friedman, 1998; Hassin et al., 2005). As you're talking with someone, you observe their nonverbal behaviors as well as what they say. They in turn observe your nonverbal behaviors.

Sometimes the boundary between this conscious and unconscious processing is blurred. That is, we have a "feeling" or "belief" about the communication situation, but we aren't sure "where" it comes from.

Unconsciously picking up the nonverbal communication of another person can be tough because it's "unconscious." Often we aren't even aware we're doing it. For example, consider the unconscious phenomenon of mimicking-explained earlier in the book,. Each of us often unconsciously mimics the nonverbal behaviors of others with whom we're talking. In other words, we copy the same nonverbal behaviors as the person with whom we're talking. If they cross their legs, we cross our legs. If they sit up straight, we do the same. Both people in the conversation may do this often without even being consciously aware of their actions. This can happen in any of our relationships or even with complete strangers.

11. Communication tools

If you're going to establish common ground connections with others, you need help in dealing with the challenges of verbal and nonverbal communications. There are two tools covered briefly earlier in the book which when emphasized will best help you do that: (1) targeted speaking and (2) nonverbal pinpointing.

Tool #1: targeted speaking

Instead of just talking or speaking, the goal is to "target" your speaking to the other person in the conversation. That is, you choose words that you believe the other person will understand. You adjust your verbal communication to help the other person in a conversation comprehend what you're sharing.

Targeting your speaking is a process which starts from the very beginning of a conversation. You may even make a judgment prior to the conversation about what language to use with each person. As the conversation progresses, you listen and observe the person. This enables you to use language that you believe the other person will understand. Based on this ongoing feedback you continue to make adjustments as needed .

Actions of targeted speaking

When you make adjustments to what you say as the conversation progresses, you're showing the person that you have a sincere interest in them and are interested in helping them understand you.

Targeting your speaking means you must engage your conscious self in monitoring the conversation. That means not only an awareness of what the other person is communicating but also an awareness of your own communication (Young, 2015).

The following actions will help you target your speaking including (1) listen and interpret, (2) ask for feedback, (3) use silence, and (4) be patient in asking questions. They are not "steps" in a process. Rather, use these as needed throughout a conversation based on whether you think the other person understands the words and language you're using.

Listen and interpret Listen carefully to the words the other person is using. Make an initial interpretation of their meaning. What are they really saying? What might be the deeper meaning behind what they're talking about? Avoid settling on your first interpretation of their words and language. Be open to considering that meaning and understanding can change throughout any conversation.

> **Example:** Your girlfriend of 3 months says she wants to talk to you about something. You're immediately concerned, but you know there's no avoiding it. She says she's feeling a bit trapped in the relationship. She thinks that seeing you every night is a bit over the top at this point in your relationship. She wonders if "you both should start seeing other people." That's the kiss of death in a relationship right next to: "Let's just be friends." But, you want to be sure that it's clear what she's proposing. So you ask her to expand on what she just said, and provide specifics as to what she wants to do. You listen carefully and make sure you have all the details on her proposal.

Ask for feedback Monitor the conversation to confirm understanding. Confirm or disconfirm your interpretations of the meaning of the other person's words and language by asking them for feedback.

> **Example:** Your boss at work loves to delegate work to you. The last time she did this, you weren't clear what she was asking you to do. The job she's apparently

delegating to you is not something you've done before. You ask her for feedback about the project. Once she provides the instruction you confirm what you think she said by rephrasing in your own words the details of the instructions.

Use silence   A reasonable amount of silence is not something to be avoided by either person in a conversation. The natural give and take of a conversation means that there will be at least some silence as people think about what's been said, and what they want to say next. It might mean that people are being respectful of the give and take of a conversation as well. Avoid the feeling that you must fill the silence with talk.

> **Example:** You're talking with your daughter who's a senior at a local college. She's indicated she wants to drop out of school and join the Peace Corps. You and your husband admire her desire to want to help in this way, but believe it's in her best interest to finish college before she does that. Your daughter is really fired up and acts like her mind is made up. You say: "Do you think it would be better to finish college before entering the Peace Corp? You father and I think it might be hard to come back and finish school after years away. What do you think?"
>
> She says that it's such a great opportunity, and that she really feels "called" to do this kind of work. Rather than argue with her you are just silent. You want to encourage her to elaborate on the reasons for her decision.

Be patient in asking questions   When you ask a question, give the other person time to answer it. People talk at different rates and process information at different speeds. Sometimes your conversational partner needs time to process what you've just said, and then make a reasonable response. Jumping in if you get impatient often just interrupts them and makes them have to start over. When you do this, you end up with a disjointed conversation. You want to listen more and jump in less.

> **Example:** Your friend Neil is a "slow" talker. He's very deliberate when he speaks. He has interesting things to share, but he takes so long to share them. In contrast to Neil, you're pretty wound up most of the time talking a mile a minute. You're adjusted to Neil because he's your best friend, but sometimes you get impatient. You feel like you want to finish his sentences. You're often guilty of interrupting him in the middle of a sentence on a regular basis. You realize that you must be patient with Neil because he's your friend and because your patience will be rewarded with interesting information. And as you think about it, Neil may also have to adjust to you talking a mile a minute.

Your goal—shared understanding

When you target your speaking, you're seeking to create a shared meaning through the language you use with others. Meaning in this case is not defined by either you or the other person. You're developing a shared understanding as the conversation progresses. This is verbal common ground connection.

As with other aspects of common ground connections, targeted speaking is about a focus on the other person. In this case, it's surrendering your need to use language with which you are more comfortable. Instead, you must use language that is comfortable for both you and the other person, and that keeps the conversation moving toward mutual understanding.

Tool #2: nonverbal pinpointing

Similar to targeted speaking, when we "pinpoint" the nonverbal behaviors of others we identify or choose specific nonverbal behaviors we observe. Once you've done that, you must then determine which of those behaviors is most relevant to understanding the other person in the present conversation. Relevant means you must consciously choose which nonverbal behaviors to process and which behaviors to disregard.

Nonverbal pinpointing helps you to organize and ultimately understand the large amount of nonverbal information you get from every conversation. Without using the pinpointing process, you can become overwhelmed by all the nonverbal behaviors communicating different things.

Really learning to pick up on all the nuances and types of nonverbal communication of others takes practice and time even with people you've known a long time. Even a close friend can change their nonverbal communication.

Actions of nonverbal pinpointing

The following "conscious" and "unconscious" methods of nonverbal pinpointing will give you the best chance of accurately interpreting and understanding the nonverbal communication of others.

Conscious processes: There are a number of "methods" you can use to consciously pinpoint the nonverbal behaviors of others: (1) always consider context, (2) use clustering, (3) use nonverbal baselines, (4) monitor comfort levels, and (5) watch for nonverbal leakage.

Method: Always consider context

When you observe the nonverbal communication of others you'll be more accurate when you consider the "context" in which those behaviors occur. That is, if someone is crying at a funeral you wouldn't think much about it. Crying isn't unusual in that situation. If someone is crying at work, you would be more likely to wonder what's wrong. Crying is usually not common in most work situations.

Method: Cluster

Often we observe one nonverbal behavior from another person and draw broad conclusions about what they're trying to communicate or what they're feeling. We jump to conclusions. It's easier and takes less time. The problem is that you can't accurately pinpoint another person's communication by observing only one nonverbal action. Your pinpointing is usually wrong because you're basing it on a fraction of the information being communicated.

Your conversational accuracy can be improved by using clustering. Clustering simply means using multiple nonverbal behaviors of the other person to try to interpret and understand them. When you observe multiple nonverbal behaviors all telling you the same thing, your interpretations are much more likely to be correct. If I observe only one nonverbal behavior of someone and then believe I know what they're thinking and feeling, I may be wrong. Clustering requires a certain amount of patience, but will result in a more accurate reading of other people's nonverbal communication.

Method: Use nonverbal baselines

A nonverbal baseline is a description of another person's nonverbal communication you've formed with each person with whom you have conversations. You have a baseline for each of the people in your life particularly people you know—friends, family, work colleagues, and others. You don't have to "start over" every time you have a conversation with someone. You use the baseline you've already established and then continue to interpret the person's nonverbal behaviors as the conversation progresses.

What are examples of baselines? One person you talk with for example might like to look right at you throughout a conversation. Another person uses a whole host of gestures. Still another person likes to stand really close to you when talking. You put together all the unique nonverbal communication actions of a particular person to create a unique baseline for that person. You use that baseline along with situational factors, context, relational factors, and common sense to get an accurate reading of the other person in every conversation.

Think of a family member with whom you have a baseline. Do they gesture a lot? Are they facially expressive? Your baseline for that family member would be a description of each area of their nonverbal communication.

Keep in mind that sometimes the baseline you establish can be "off." People's communication can change. Thus, it's a good idea to be open to modifying or updating your baselines.

Understanding baselines is particularly important when people aren't communicating according to the baseline you've established for them. When that happens, you know something's wrong or that the person isn't telling you the whole truth. Try to determine what's going on with that person in your present conversation if it "seems" the person isn't communicating according to your baseline of them. It could be also that you'll need to just "update" your baseline.

You develop baselines even with people you've just met. Admittedly, your baseline with a new acquaintance might be pretty general, but you still use it to make sense of them and their communication. As you get to know the person better, you adapt your baseline as needed (Taylor, Body Language Matters website).

Method: Monitor comfort levels

When you communicate with people you want to avoid making them feel uncomfortable. You can't communicate effectively or create a common ground connection with someone who's distracted.

To ensure there's a conversational comfort level you need to not only monitor the nonverbal communication of the other person, but also your own nonverbal communication. Does the other person seem to be irritated, distracted or uncomfortable? And are you doing anything in the conversation that may be creating those negative feelings? If you like to stand very close to people when you talk for example, you may inadvertently make the other person feel uncomfortable if they like a little more space. If the other person continues to back away from you while you're talking, you may be the cause. Balance observing the other person with an awareness of your own nonverbal communication to keep the conversation "comfortable."

Method: Watch for nonverbal "leakage"

The other person's "leakage"

Nonverbal leakage occurs when you believe someone is inadvertently communicating something through their nonverbal communication. You're not 100% sure, but you believe that the person is saying one thing, but their nonverbal behaviors are communicating something else. Their true feelings are "leaking" out.

If you're in a regular conversation, and you believe the other person's real feelings are "leaking," what should you do? The person may have very good reasons for hiding their true feelings or opinions. Maybe the person is embarrassed by the discussion, they don't want to reveal their true feelings, or they may be deliberately lying to you.

The best suggestion for resolving this situation is to compassionately confirm your suspicions. You could be wrong. The leakage might be the result of other factors like context, distractions, or the other person's communication style, and be totally unrelated to the present conversation. If you end up wrongly accusing the person, you break down any possibly of a common ground connection with that person. You may have damaged the long-term relationship as well.

Your own "leakage"

You obviously have to be aware of your own leakage as well. If for example you don't like a particular person for whatever reason, your nonverbal behaviors might inadvertently communicate that without you even realizing it. Maybe you don't look at them, daydream, or look bored. All these behaviors will give the other person the impression you don't really want to talk to them. Your real feelings are "leaking out" to the other person (Shen et al., 2021).

Let's say you're in a job interview about which you're very nervous. During the interview you're able to control the top part of your body. You sit up straight, avoid distracting mannerisms, look right at the interviewer, and in general work to appear calm and collected. Inside however, you're a wreck. Eventually your nervousness gets so bad that it "leaks out." That is, your legs start shaking uncontrollably. You put your hands on the tops of your legs, but it doesn't seem to help. Your leg shaking is an outward manifestation of your inner nervousness.

You may not be able to consciously stop your legs from shaking. You may not even realize it, but the interviewer may be able to see that they are. Even if at some point you become consciously aware that your legs are shaking, you may not be able to stop them. You're just too nervous. Your inner nervousness had "leaked" to your legs.

The establishment of a common ground connection with another person has to be based on honesty between the people involved. Whether it's the other person or yourself "successful" communication is based on "honest' communication between the people involved. If there's significant "leakage," by one or both people, there's too much deception going on.

12. Conclusion

One of the tenets of this book is that changing our personal and societal communications will start to "heal" the many divisions currently in the United States and the world. This change must start with the communication we use most often in our daily lives—verbal and nonverbal communications. How we use our verbal and nonverbal skills can sometimes be the cause of our problems but can also be the solution in relating to others. Further, if we're going to come together as a world we need to use our basic verbal and nonverbal communication to bridge the many current divisions.

As the name implies, common ground connections are about bringing all.

Bibliography

Alang, S., McAlpine, D., McCreedy, E., & Hardeman, R. (2017). Police brutality and Black health: Setting the agenda for public health scholars. *American Journal of Public Health, 107*(5), 662–665.

Allyn, B. (2019, September 26). The 'OK' hand gesture is now listed as a symbol of hate. *NPR.*

Anderson, D., Stuart, M., Abadi, M., & Gal, S. (2019, January 5). 5 everyday hand gestures that can get you in serious trouble outside the US. *Insider.*

Calin, A. (2019, July 25). Nonverbal communication in a digital world. *Hubgets.*

Carlson, A. (2022, April 30). Difference between verbal communication and nonverbal communication. *Difference.*

Cherry, K. (2021, July 28). Types of nonverbal communication. *Verywell Mind.*

Cowen, A. S., & Keltner, D. (2017). Self-report captures 27 distinct categories of emotion bridged by continuous gradients. *Proceedings of the National Academy of Science USA, 114*(38), E7900–E7909.

Crossman, A. (2020, February 3). An overview of labeling theory. *Thought Co.*

Depaulo, B. M., & Friedman, H. S. (1998). Nonverbal communication. In D. T. Gilbert, S. T. Fiske, & G. Lindzey (Eds.), *The handbook of social psychology* (pp. 3–40). McGraw-Hill.

DiGiulio, S. (2018, January 9). In good company: Why we need other people to be happy. *NBC News, Better.*

DuPraw, M. E., & Axner, M. (2022). Toward a more perfect union in an age of diversity, working on common cross-cultural challenges. *PBS.*

Fry, D. P. (1993). Conflict resolution: Cross-cultural perspectives. *Journal of Aggressive Behavior, 19*(4), 313–315.

Gratis, B. (2022, February 4). Overcoming language barriers to communication. *Typetalk, blog.*

Halcrow, N. (2019, May 31). I'm sorry! Was that rude? Hand gestures around the world. *CultureWizard RW3.*

Haltiwanger, J. (2014, October 7). We are all human: 10 labels we need to stop using to describe people. *Elite Daily.*

Hassin, R. R., Uleman, J. S., & Bargh, J. A. (Eds.). (2005). *The new unconscious.* Oxford University Press.

Holt-Lunstad, J., Smith, T. B., Baker, M., Harris, T., & Stephenson, D. (2015, March 11). Loneliness and social isolation as risk factors for mortality: A meta-analytic review. *Sage Journals, 10*(2). https://doi.org/10.1177/1745691614568352

Kelly, L. (2017, July 23). Is your vocabulary higher than the average adult? *DirectExpose, The Outside World.*

London, J. (2018, June 27). 70+ big words that will make you feel smart. *Thought Catalog.*

Matthews, H. M. (2014). *The concise oxford dictionary of linguistics.* Oxford University Press, 443 pp.

Neeley, T. (2012, May). Global business speaks English. *Harvard Business Review.*

Nordquist, R. (2018, December 6). Paralinguistics (paralanguage), glossary of grammatical and rhetorical terms. *ThoughtCo.*

Nordquist, R. (2019, July 17). Paralinguistics (paralanguage). *Thought Co.*

Nunez, D. (2014). War of the words: Aliens, immigrants, citizens and the language of exclusion. *Brigham Young University Law Review, 2013*, 1517–1562.

Passel, J. S., & Cohn, D. (2017). As Mexican share declined, U.S. unauthorized immigrant population fell in 2015 below recession level. *Pew Research Center.*

Romey, B. (2021, January 12). Decoding the hate symbols seen at the Capitol insurrection. *National Geographic.*

Rucker, J. M., Murphy, M. C., & Quintanilla, V. D. (2019). The immigrant labeling effect: The role of immigrant group labels in prejudice against noncitizens. *Group Processes and Intergroup Relations, 22*(8), 1139–1160.

Seigel, J. (2021, April 8). Spotting a liar isn't as easy as you think. Here's why verbal cues may be better indicators than nonverbal signs that someone is lying. *Insider.*

Shen, X., Fan, G., Niu, C., & Chen, Z. (2021, June 8). Catching a liar through facial expression of fear. *Frontiers in Psychology.*

Sreenivasan, S., & Weinberger, L. E. (2016, December 14). Why we need each other. Loneliness is a negative condition resulting from a state of aloneness. *Psychology Today.*

Stroud, M. (2018, August 29). What does hate look like? A guide to symbols used by hate groups in PA. *PublicSource.*

The ThoughtCo Team. (2019, January 4). The top 10 French gestures. *ThoughtCo.*

Thuillier, M. (2019, February 28). For immigrants, labels simplify necessary complexities. *The Daily Northwestern.*

Tollshein, E. (2019, March 30). Who are you without the labels you've been given by society? *Medium.*

Vaughn, B. D. (2020, June 11). It's not just a handshake: How COVID-19 will change Black greetings and the DAP. *Complex.*

Watzlawick, B.-B., & Jackson, D. (1967). Some tentative axioms of communication. In *Pragmatics of human communication: A study of interactional patterns, pathologies and paradoxes.* W.W. Norton.

Wezowski, K. (2018, September 18). How to get better at reading people from different cultures. *Harvard Business Review.*

Young, G. (2015, April 15). A 6-step program for improving your communication skills. *Entrepreneur.*

Zetter, K. (2003, September 2). What a half smile really means. *Wired.*

6

LISTENING ENERGETICALLY

There's currently a strange phenomenon occurring in the United States and the world. It seems we've largely stopped listening to one another. We've made up our minds about things and have become more and more entrenched in our beliefs. Many are not interested in listening to anyone's opinion anymore unless it agrees with their own. Listening is sharing. We're not sharing.

This lack of listening has made some of the divisions that already exist in the world more pronounced. In other cases, it has also created divisions where none existed.

DOI:10.4324/9781003357049-6

How does all this manifest itself in America? People are only listening to like-minded people. They join groups which believe what they do. The Southern Poverty Law Center hate and extremism report found that there were 733 such groups in 2021. This is a decline from 1,021 groups in 2018. Most experts believe, however, that the beliefs of many of these groups have gone mainstream so that the reasons for certain groups no longer exists. Further, much of the hate activity—including recruiting—occurs online (Fatherree, 2022).

These hate groups aren't listening to any other perspectives. Their opinion becomes what you would call "entrenched." They're not really interested in hearing anything that contradicts their viewpoint. Entrenched beliefs are very resistant to change.

How people and groups with entrenched beliefs respond is different from other groups as well. They're much more likely to respond strongly or sometimes violently to people who don't agree with them. Why is this so? When I have an entrenched belief, it's basically the core of who I am. When people who believe differently than I do confront me with a different way of looking at something, I may thus believe that they're attacking the very core of who I am. I'm no longer listening to them. I'm spending my mental energies determining how best to counter what they're saying. I have to defend myself.

We need to find a way to unify all people whether they have entrenched beliefs or not. That means we must make an effort to listen to all perspectives and all people. More and more people seem to have gravitated to a single, unchangeable point of view.

Common ground connections and listening

Focus on the other person

To be an effective listener you must adopt a core principle of common ground connections—focus on the other person. Focusing on the other person through your listening is tough because you just can't stay focused all the time. Your mind is too active and there are always too many distractions. You have to help yourself by putting your full energies into listening. You have to put your self-interests and what you want to talk about on hold while you're listening. You can't focus on yourself and the other person at the same time. That doesn't work.

You can't be completely selfless either. That isn't how you're built. But you can work to make the other person the center of your attention when you're engaged in a conversation. Your goal is to not only understand what the other person is really saying but also get an idea of "who" they are as a person and why they believe what they do.

Your reward for using your listening energies to focus on the other person is that you'll develop a very personal bond called a common ground connection with the other person. When you take this perspective, that person is more likely to listen to you as well.

When you attempt to communicate with people who don't share your beliefs, focusing on the other person can be even tougher. In many cases, you don't want to focus on them or listen to them at all. Their views are just too offensive. If I'm a Black man, the idea that I would be able to talk with or have anything in common with a member of the Klu Klux Klan would be too bizarre to accept.

But focusing on the other person through listening is exactly what we have to do if we're going to bring people and this world together. First, each of us needs to determine a good reason for wanting to communicate with another person whom we basically don't like or respect. What's the real motivation? What can you accomplish long term by considering their point of view? Can you make a situation better? Can you learn something? Could you change their point of view?

Dealing with people who are so different from you requires a mental toughness on your part. When you start talking with them, you may go into "mental shock." What they're saying may be so offensive and unreasonable to you that emotions of anger and disbelief may flood your brain. This flood may prevent you from thinking in any reasoned way. For example, if you're a gay person, and the person with whom you're trying to communicate is completely anti-gay, you've got your hands full.

But each of us needs to get past this mental anxiety spike in order to really keep listening. Only in this way can you really focus on that person and what they believe. Even if it's only one thing, you can build on that one point. You may not agree with them about much, but if you can agree with them on some parts of the issue you have a start. Then you keep building on that partial agreement as you continue to seek a common ground connection with them. The building of common ground connections may just end up changing minds—yours and theirs.

Make the other person feel good about themselves

With listening you can take this focus on the other person to the next level by seeking to make the person feel good about themselves. That is, when you're talking with someone recognize instances when the other person did something that was really good in or outside the conversation. Maybe they resolved a problem with someone. In that case, you might say: "Wow, you really used your problem solving skills to resolve that situation with your sister! I didn't think anyone could fix that. You did!" Or maybe they got a job with a company that's really tough to get. You might say: "It sounds like you really nailed that interview. It's really hard to get interviewed by that company. Gimme five."

You don't need to lie or stretch the truth. Just listen to the other person and stay alert for times when the person really did something good. If they did, share your admiration and enthusiasm for their actions.

When you do this you'll find that the other person is almost taken aback by your gesture. They'll think: "Yeah, I guess I did do a good job. I hadn't realized how well I did." They'll feel good about themselves, the conversation, and you for pointing out their efforts. You'll feel the same way. In a sense, you and the other person have created a natural common ground connection around one person's success. It causes both people to step back and take in a mutually created sensation of really celebrating success.

Can you imagine using this "make the other person feel good about themselves" action with someone with whom you're having a serious conflict, a racist, or even a white supremacist? It would probably take them off guard initially. But it might be the start of having a more productive dialogue with a person you find offensive. Everyone has something they do well in their life. Everyone has friends. Most love their families. You would probably learn something new about them by approaching them and any issues between you from a more positive perspective. This new information might be just what you need to create a common ground connection with someone you thought you never could.

There will always be things on which we don't agree with others even close friends and family. But, instead of focusing only on our differences, building common ground connections helps us build on commonalities. Making the other person feel good about themselves is one tool to help you with that.

Your listening challenges

Think about all the times you're listening to someone. Are there times when you're distracted, tired, or worried about something? Have you realized in some conversations that you're not focused or easily distracted? Maybe you've been "caught" daydreaming?

The following are challenges to your listening effectiveness. By becoming more aware of these challenges, you'll be better able to overcome them.

Specific challenges

We all have short attention spans

One of the most important listening challenges we face is that we have short attention spans. This is important because in order to listen effectively we must "pay attention."

Some research indicates that the adult attention span is only 3–24 seconds. Other authors contend we don't really know how long a person's attention span is. When the 3–24 second figure is quoted, it doesn't mean much because there are too many factors involved. For example, is the topic interesting? If you're interested, you're more likely to work hard to pay attention. How do you feel about the person with whom you're having a conversation? If you don't like the person, you're less likely to put in the effort to pay attention to them.

At least part of the reason for what can be a short attention span is that's there so much going on around us. You can't process everything. There's just too much. So as you try to pay attention to one thing, something else distracts you. You best deal with this by accepting that you must focus on what you decide is most important for you.

Research in the area of human attention span is called divided attention research. The research studies often use headphones to play one message in a person's ear, and a second, different message in the person's other ear. The goal of the subject is to remember one or both messages as best as he/she can. It's similar to what you might do at home. Are you doing your taxes while watching television? To which are you more likely to pay attention? Or perhaps your children are listening to rock music while doing their homework. Can they really do that?

Research has generally found that subjects who heard different messages in their ears tended to focus on one message to the exclusion of the other. This meant, for example, that subjects could remember 70–80% of the message on which they focused, but only about 20% of the other message.

So it appears that you really can't pay attention to two things at once. You may think you can, but what you're really doing is switching back and forth from one thing to another. Eventually, you're only listening to one thing. Trying to listen to someone while also worrying about a friend who's sick, being concerned about getting your "to do" list done by the end of the day, and thinking about how hungry you are just doesn't work. It prevents you from really thinking about the conversation and processing important details of what's being shared in real time.

You can imagine what all this means for your listening and understanding. If you think you can listen to someone while checking your cell phone or doing anything else besides paying attention, you may end up not processing much of anything. It doesn't say much about your interest in talking with that person either. If you want to establish common ground connections, you must focus on the other person as fully as you can without making them compete with your distractions.

If you still feel like you can multi-task during a conversation, try multi-tasking the next time you're with a close friend. After the conversation, ask them for their reaction to your listening. You may believe you were able to talk to them and still do a bunch of other things during the conversation. They may tell you otherwise.

We're easily distracted

Distraction is simply letting your attention wander from what the other person is saying. There are two types of distractions—internal and external. External distractions include noise, interruptions, other people, and anything else happening in your environment that prevents you from focusing on the other person.

Internal distractions include fatigue, worry, and anxiety. You can often eliminate outside distractions, for example, by going to a different place where it's quieter. That's not always true with internal distractions.

The goal is not to eliminate distractions. It's hard to imagine that anyone could ever do that. The goal is to manage those times when you're distracted. If you find yourself daydreaming, for example, just bring yourself back to the conversation and re-focus your efforts.

Each of us does this every day. For example, you may work in a busy, noisy office. You've learned over time how to focus on a conversation you're having with your boss within that environment. You learn how to tune out most of the distractions. At some point, it may be a good idea to go to a quieter area, but generally you deal with the situation as is.

Preview of chapter

The purpose of this chapter is to provide you with background on what's really going on when you listen. An understanding of these aspects of listening is important because they are at the core of creating common ground connections. The sections of the chapter are as follows:

1. Listening basics
2. Your mind, listening, and common ground connections
3. Intentional listening skills
4. Memory and listening
5. We often focus too much on ourselves
6. Actions of listening
7. Changing the world one person at a time

The information covered in this chapter is not "prescriptive." The suggestions given are just "suggestions." To best use the information, you need to determine how you can best integrate the suggestions into your current listening style.

1. Listening basics

What is listening?

Listening is a gift you give another person. You're saying what they have to say is important. They understand you're trying your best to understand what they're sharing and "where they're coming from." You're putting them ahead of yourself for that moment in time.

Each of us needs to feel we've been heard. This meets our basic need for inclusion and connection with other human beings. Listening is really "sharing." This can be tough. We tend to be focused on ourselves. That's our default setting. It's often hard to change that setting. Plus, our culture rewards talkers. There's rarely a reward for the listener.

When you unselfishly listen to the other person, they appreciate it. You show a respect for the other person that's reciprocated as the conversation progresses.

The reward for this sharing perspective is that you'll consistently begin to have conversations that are mutually beneficial. You'll have the information you need to create common ground connections in an increasing number of your conversations. You and the other people with whom you have conversations will be more likely to stay engaged too.

You spend a lot of time listening

Each of us spends a tremendous amount of our time listening to others. Estimates of the amount of time are usually around 50% of total communication time. Some believe that adults on average spend nearly 6 hours each day in listening.

In reality, these estimates may not tell us much. The amount of time you spend listening really depends on an incredible amount of factors including you as a person, what you happen to be doing on a given day, with whom you interact, and a number of other factors. These factors are too varied to enable us to meaningful assign a number to the "amount" of time spent listening. What's important are not the percentages but the general agreement that we spend a large portion of our time listening.

How did you learn to listen?

You probably learned how to listen from your parents or a caregiver who raised you. If they were "good listeners," you learned good listening habits which you probably continue to use today. You developed a listening "style" based on what you saw them do. You used your own experiences as you grew up to modify that style as needed. Regardless of your situation, however, as you grew older you learned to listen in a way that seemed to make sense to you.

Unfortunately, not everyone was brought up by people who could listen well. Some people weren't listened to at all or were ridiculed and degraded. These people had no "model" to follow in learning to listen. They may have realized what they didn't like or what not to do, but that was about it.

Further, your listening ability is more than just your own specific skill set. Listening is really an interpersonal activity. Measuring your personal listening ability must always be done within the context of each conversation. You may notice this yourself in your various relationships. You're probably a better listener with some people than others based on closeness to the person, length of the relationship, and other factors. For example, you probably listen with energy to your brother with whom you're close. He's supported you and been a good friend as well as a brother ever since you can remember.

Are you a good listener?

When asked whether they're effective listeners, it's not unusual for people to rate themselves as high as 90%. Yet those same people who rated themselves highly also admitted that sometimes they don't listen well.

What will help you to determine how good a listener you are is to critically evaluate how you listen now in your varied conversations. Do you generally understand the points made by the people with whom you talk? Do people seem frustrated with you because you're not able to understand them?

What's more important than your self-rating of your listening are the opinions of those people with whom you have conversations. Your listening effectiveness is mostly determined by how other people rate you. What you have to guard against is the tendency to believe you're a better listener than you are.

2. Your mind, listening, and common ground connections

Research into how the brain functions between two people in a conversation has shown that the listeners' and speaker's brain responses can be very similar. These studies indicate that as a conversation continues and both people begin to understand one another, the brain responses are even more similar. Some researchers label this latter finding "brain coupling" or "brain synchrony." Regardless of what you call it, it's simply sharing a mindset with another person during a conversation. You've probably had the experience of really being able to tune in to another person's thinking when talking to them. This is an indication that you established a common ground connection.

How does this work? You might think to yourself during a conversation: "I wonder what the other person is really thinking about?" This is part of your efforts at focusing on the other person. In this case, you're more focused on what the other person may be thinking as opposed to what they're saying. You try to verify your perceptions by continuing the conversation and getting feedback from them.

There are two tools that can help with your mental efforts in listening to others. They're an integral part of being able to create common ground connections. You just naturally use these skills, but you can enhance your listening by becoming more aware of these tools. The two tools are (1) thought speed and (2) empathy.

Thought speed

One of the main tools that will help you listen to others is your thought speed advantage. What is thought speed? Thought speed is the difference between one person's speed of speaking and the other person's speed of listening to the information they're hearing. Typically, a person speaks about 125–150 words per minute. Listeners can mentally process information at least twice that speed with some estimates as high as 400–500 words per minute.

This means you theoretically have "extra" time to consciously process the information in a conversation and still listen effectively. It may be fractions of a second, but those fractions add up in the course of a conversation. All those fractions are your thought speed "advantage."

If you use this advantage productively, it can be a tremendous tool. You might think about what the other person has just said, search for deeper meanings, or recall a similar experience you've had. You still listen. You're just processing the conversation more thoroughly and from everyone's perspective because you have this "extra" time at your disposal.

How does thought speed work in a conversation? Let's say you're having a conversation with your father about his plans to retire. He's describing the retirement community in which he wants to live in Palm Springs, California. You're thinking about what he's saying and also trying to visually picture what that community might look like. You continue to listen to him, but you also have "time" to process your own thoughts on his situation. Although you can't do both of these actions at the same time, your mind can switch between them so quickly that they appear to happen simultaneously.

Unfortunately, we sometimes use our thought speed unproductively. Because the people with whom we regularly interact are talking slowly in relation to how fast our minds can work, we let ourselves be distracted, daydream, and in other ways fail to stay with the conversation. For example, a close friend is telling you about her vacation to Nassau, Bahamas. As you settle into the conversation, your mind begins to wander and you start thinking about your own vacation to Nassau last year. The more you do this, the less likely you are to listen to her experiences.

Because your mind works so quickly in relation to the conversational speed of others, it's natural to "go off" to Nassau at times in a conversation. The problem is not that you "go off," but that you don't "come back." It takes mental discipline to control how you use your thought speed time. If you daydream, think only about what you're going to say next, carry on a mental debate on the person's outfit, and do other unproductive mental activities, you're wasting your thought speed advantage.

Taking advantage of this tool enables you to better focus on the other person and the information in the conversation. You're using your mental skills to their fullest. When you do this, you have more information with which to understand others and thus create common ground connections with them.

What are some ways you can take advantage of your thought speed time?

In order to take advantage of your thought speed time, you must discipline yourself to "stay with" every conversation. Consider these suggestions:

Weigh the information the other person is presenting. Do you really understand it? If you don't, you know to ask a question. Do you agree with it? If you're not sure balance your thinking between your own thinking while still "hearing the other person out."

Review and summarize. At various points in the conversation, review and mentally summarize what the person has just said. This not only helps you make sense of it, but also helps you determine what questions you want to ask. You can even share your summary with the person to see if you've understood what they've said correctly. You might say something like: "So what I heard you saying is . . ."

Look for deeper meaning. Try to determine if there is a deeper meaning to what the person is saying. Is there a consistent theme that's running through their communication? For example the person with whom you're talking is sharing their frustration with a person at work. You're not sure whether it's a significant frustration for them or if they're just blowing off steam. To help you do this you must not only listen to what they're saying, but also read their nonverbal behaviors (Nichols & Stevens, 1957).

Thought speed gives you the chance to think about a conversation while you're having it. It enables you to not only process information, but also really think about what other people are saying. It helps you as a communicator because it helps you process the information available more accurately so that your responses are more on target.

Empathy

A major factor in creating common ground connections through your listening is your ability to demonstrate empathy. We're born with an innate ability to demonstrate empathy toward others which we continue to use throughout our life. There is a separate chapter on empathy, but this section highlights how you consciously and unconsciously demonstrate empathy toward others.

Conscious empathy. Most of us make a conscious effort to demonstrate empathy. When a friend of yours gets divorced, you talk with her to help her get through the trauma. When your daughter loses her soccer game, you encourage her to keep trying. The extent to which you demonstrate empathy is based on a number of factors including your relationship with the other person, what the person is sharing, and other factors unique to a given conversation.

Demonstrating empathy toward another person can be as simple as giving others the chance to talk, encouraging them to share with you, and showing them that you're paying attention to them. When you demonstrate empathy you show the other person that you care about them as a person and are interested in what they have to say.

We don't always consciously use our empathy skills in conversations however. People differ in their ability and willingness to demonstrate empathy for others. The majority of people seem to have a concern for other people even though it might not always show. On the other hand people sometimes don't respond to the emotions of others at all.

If you don't have at least a minimal empathy for another person, it will be nearly impossible to listen to them. Why? Because basically you're not interested in what the other person has to say. And because of that, you don't put out much effort to listen and understand them.

Fortunately, as covered earlier in the book, effort is more important than effectiveness with empathy. That is, the very fact that you listened to another person and tried to understand them is more important than whether you were "accurate" or not. Relatively unsophisticated strategies might do the best job of comforting another in a specific situation. You can't be "wrong" only absent in your efforts.

Unconscious empathy. Sometimes we demonstrate empathy without deliberately thinking about it. Consider these two aspects of unconscious empathy: 1) emotional contagion, and 2) the chameleon effect.

Emotional contagion. Have you ever been watching television when you suddenly saw someone cut themselves or got injured in a car accident? Even though you're sitting comfortably on your sofa, you still may have winced or cringed at the sight of someone else's pain. Or you're at a wedding of a friend you've known your whole life. Your friend starts to cry out of happiness. You automatically follow suit and join in. Why does this happen? We seem to have an innate and, in many cases, automatic reaction to other people's experiences—good and bad.

Emotional contagion is the tendency each of us has to pick up on the emotions of the people with whom we're communicating. Because the other person is feeling a certain emotion you often start to feel the same emotion. People are affected by and affect others with whom they interact. Modern brain scanning technology has revealed, that the same areas of your brain often become activated not only when we experience a sensation or feeling ourselves, but also when we see other people experience it.

Chameleon effect. As covered previously, people seem to copy or mimic the person with whom they're talking without intending to and without realizing that they have done so. This phenomenon is called "the chameleon effect" (Chartrand & Bargh, 1999). For example research has shown that often two people who are talking can often mirror each other's nonverbal behaviors. If one person crosses their arms, the other person crosses their arms as well. If one person begins to slouch in their seat, the other person does the same thing. Upon follow-up, the subjects in the study weren't even aware that they were doing it.

3. Intentional listening skills

The following skills are not "natural" or "innate" skills which everyone possesses. They're skills you learn and develop over time in your communication with others. Some of these skills you may already use with a great degree of success. Others are skills you might not "normally" use or may not have even tried before. What's important is that these skills are the perfect complement to your listening efforts in creating common ground connections.

> **Skill #1: put in the effort to listen**
> **Skill #2: be flexible and adaptable in the moment**
> **Skill #3: use your best verbal and nonverbal skills**
> **Skill #4: seek self and other feedback**
> **Skill #5: be mindful**
> **Skill #6: demonstrate sensitivity**

Skill #1: put in the effort to listen

More than anything, listening is about putting in the effort to understand another person.

Listening is hard work. At the end of a workday, you may be exhausted even though you basically sat at your desk all day. This is because you still exerted mental and physical energies in listening and interacting with co-workers.

We don't always want to put in the effort required to really listen in each conversation. It's too exhausting.

Effort in listening means listening "energetically" and with your whole self. As part of common ground connections, it means completely focusing on the present conversation and the person with whom you're speaking. It's a state of mind that requires you to "lock in" mentally to another person. You seek to develop a high level of concentration and focus. It requires physical exertion as you use your nonverbal behaviors to support the other person through eye contact, nodding, and other nonverbal actions. It's not a list of steps to follow. It can't be because each conversation is unique requiring a slightly different emphasis.

Skill #2: be flexible and adaptable at the moment

When you talk with someone are you flexible and adaptable? That is, are you willing to change how you speak or phrase something in order to help the other person understand? Or are you rigid and inflexible expecting the other person to adapt to you?

You already adapt your listening to other people all the time. You probably work with someone who likes to talk a lot. You don't particularly like talking to them, but she's on your team so you can't really avoid it. You learn to listen to her as best you can. Or you find the Vice President of your department really boring. But, by necessity, you try to listen to pick up key parts of his message, particularly those points that might impact you. If you have a 4–5-year-old son or daughter, you modify your communication with them. Maybe you use a simpler vocabulary or talk slightly slower. They just don't have the communication experience or sophistication you've developed through the years.

Adaptability can be tough in at least two situations: (1) a person who has a perspective with which you don't agree and (2) a person who brings out emotions of anger or frustration. In these cases, we have a natural tendency to quit listening to them once they say something with which we disagree. At some level, this just makes sense. One, you don't want to hear anything more about what they're talking about. And two, once they've set you off you're only thinking about how you're going to confront them with the error of their ways.

If you want to establish a common ground connection with someone, you need to consciously decide to be flexible in your ideas and expectations regardless of your personal feelings toward someone. As you practice this, you'll naturally become better at adjusting to every person (Tan, June 20, 2016).

Each of us makes the decision to be flexible in our communication or to be rigid and inflexible. You'll be a better communicator if you're perceived to adjust to others in conversations. People with whom you talk appreciate the fact that you're willing to adjust your communication with them. When you're adaptable and flexible, you're really using slightly different listening styles for each of the people with whom you interact.

Adaptability increases your chances of creating common ground connections for a number of reasons:

> **More information.** Because you do what you need to do to adjust to the other person, you'll pick up more information and more accurate information. You take the information you process from the conversation, and match it with your own perspectives. In this way you find commonalities much easier than if you only operated from your own perspective.
>
> **You'll improve your basic listening skills.** You'll be more flexible in how you communicate with others. You'll do what you need to get through to others.
>
> **You demonstrating sincere effort.** You create a conversation in which the other person understands that you're really working hard to understand them and their perspectives. They appreciate your efforts.

Skill #3: use your best verbal and nonverbal skills

There is a full chapter in this book on enhancing your targeted speaking and non-verbal pinpointing skills in establishing common ground connections. The two tools covered in that chapter are briefly reviewed here because of their impact on listening effectiveness.

Verbal tool: targeted speaking

Targeting your speaking is a process which starts from the very beginning of a conversation. You make a judgment prior to the conversation about what language to use with each person. As the conversation progresses, you energetically listen and observe the person's nonverbal communication. This enables you to consciously use language that you believe the other person will understand. Based on this ongoing feedback, you continue to make adjustments as needed.

You "target" your speaking all the time. You're usually successful at it as well. For example, when you're explaining a new machine process to one of your staff, you make sure you define all parts of the process. You may talk slower at some points in your instructions, and you continually ask whether they understand. If the person isn't following you or they admit they don't understand, you change the words and language you're using.

You do this to a lesser extent in every conversation. You always monitor whether the other person in a conversation is "following you" with the words and language you're using. If you believe a certain term is new to the other person based on a puzzled look on their face or something they say, you define that term. This is important because if you use a word like "epistemology" and the other person has no idea what you're talking about, all communication basically stops. The other person is no longer listening to you. They're "stuck" on what the heck does "epistemology" mean.

Nonverbal tool: pinpointing

To be successful in creating common ground connections, you need a process to help you deal with the complex nature of the nonverbal communication of others. That process is called nonverbal pinpointing. Nonverbal pinpointing is identifying specific nonverbal behaviors you observe and determining which of those behaviors is most relevant to understanding that person in the present conversation. Relevant means you must consciously choose which nonverbal behaviors to process and which behaviors to disregard based on what you need to understand them. This is necessary because there are just too many nonverbal behaviors in any conversation to process in any meaningful way.

Nonverbal pinpointing helps you to organize and ultimately understand the large amount of nonverbal information you get from every conversation. Without using the pinpointing process, you'd become overwhelmed.

Really learning to pick up on all the nuances and types of nonverbal communication of others takes practice and time even with people you've known a long time. Even a close friend can change how they communicate using their nonverbal behaviors.

Skill #4: seek self and other feedback

During a conversation, you can never be 100% sure of what the other person is thinking or feeling. The only way to be sure is to ask them. You need to confirm your perceptions and understanding you've gleaned from your listening. This is really the only way you can determine if you and the other person are understanding one another. Seeking feedback is also the only way to know whether you've established a common ground connection.

Skill #5: be mindful

Have you been talking to a friend and suddenly realize you haven't heard a word they said for the last 5 minutes? This is particularly a challenge when at some point they ask you: "What do you think?" Since you haven't been listening, you have to scramble to get them to at least paraphrase what they just said. Or you're in a staff meeting at work. You're bored. You naturally start thinking about something else like all the work at your desk. Someone says something in the meeting that brings you back to the meeting, but you realize you've been "off" for quite a while. You realize you're very vulnerable if the group wants your opinion on what's just been discussed.

If you're like most people you have these and other escapes all the time. There's nothing wrong with it. But, if you're going to be an effective listener you have to "manage," this tendency we all have to be distracted. In some ways, you have to learn to take an interest in the "uninteresting."

Practicing mindfulness is one method that can help you with this. Simply, mindfulness means being fully focused and attentive in the conversation in which you're engaged.

When you are mindless, you're on "automatic pilot" and expending very little effort. When you're mindful, you're open to all the emotions, thoughts, and sensations you're experiencing moment to moment as the conversation is occurring. You suspend your preconceived notions of the other person and the topic of discussion. You try to put judgments and prejudices aside. You think through the situation in order to focus on the skills you possess that will best enable you to the conversation create common ground connections.

By practicing mindfulness, you calmly observe your sensations, thoughts, and feelings as if you were externally watching your self. You get the sense that you're standing outside of your own mind watching the conversation (Schwartz & Begley, 2002). You in essence become a hidden observer of what's going on in the conversation.

When you become a mindful listener, you manage all the internal noise you normally experience in your mind. But, as the conversation progresses, an interesting phenomenon happens. You also quiet the internal noise in your conversational partner and in the conversation itself. This means that both people are more likely to just be themselves and communicate honestly because they're more relaxed.

Skill #6: demonstrate sensitivity

Interpersonal sensitivity means that you're open to perceiving and responding to the emotions of others in a conversation through their verbal and nonverbal communications. You develop this sensitivity to the communication of others over time. You might have some missteps as you develop this skill. For example, you might say some things that help, but you might make it worse for the other person. You want to avoid denying their feelings, telling them what to do, or changing the subject by relating a similar situation in which you've found yourself. You'll be less likely to be insensitive if you always center on the person and their situation.

Sometimes, when we're trying to support someone, your presence is all that is needed. You might think to yourself: "What do I say? How can I help them? There's got to be something I can do." There may not be anything to say or do—just being there is the best you can do. And just being there is a lot. There are times when nothing needs to be said—just being with them is all that you can do and the best thing at that moment for the person you're comforting.

4. Memory and listening

Since you can't attend to everything going on around you, you have to choose some information and ignore other information. Primarily you use three mental skills to help you: (1) selective attention, (2) selective exposure, and (3) selective retention.

These natural listening skills can be tremendously useful in picking out the most important information in a given conversation. But sometimes these skills can also skew the information you take in. They can be biased and limit you in what you internalize and understand, but without them you'd be overwhelmed and confused.

Selective attention

This means you pay attention to what stands out or what you think is important. When you're at a party, for example, there may be a lot going on. Everyone's talking, people are eating, and generally there's a lot of noise. In spite of all this, you're able to focus on the story your date is sharing and for the most part tune out everything else.

Selective exposure

This concept means your tendency to look for and attend to information that confirms your current beliefs and ideas. The people who call you "friend" are probably similar to you and share your opinions. You watch television programs that support your opinions. You tend to avoid people who don't think like you do. If you're a conservative Republican, you probably listen to Fox News. They generally support a right-wing perspective. If I'm a liberal independent, I would avoid watching Fox News. That news would not only challenge my beliefs but also just irritate me.

The idea of selective exposure can be very strong. It's been shown that even when people are presented with undeniable contradictory evidence, they may deny it even to the point of pretending not to hear the information.

Consider deniers of the coronavirus. Some never wore masks. Others got very angry when they were required to take precautions like wearing a mask. Despite clear evidence that we are still years away from the COVID-19 pandemic being over, many people don't take any precautions (Collins, 2022).

Selective retention

Selective retention is remembering only certain aspects of a past situation based on the impact of that event on you. When we process information in a conversation, we pass what we experience through our own personal filters. These filters can be biased and even inaccurate. What you remember is not always a completely accurate view of what happened to you.

After we've broken up with someone, we often begin to miss them and consider trying to reconnect with that person. We remember all the good times. We conveniently forget the times when that person lied to us and went out with other people.

These three memory aspects can help us to make sense of conversations. They can help us select what we believe is most important and what we should ignore. We just need to keep in the mind that they can also skew and distort our interpretations.

5. We often focus too much on ourselves

A basic part of creating common ground connections is to focus on the other person. It's the opposite of being selfish and self-centered. When you're self-centered, you doom yourselves to your own perspective. You don't think much about the other person. They know it too.

More than anything else, poor listening is about being selfish. You care more about yourself and what you have to say than the other person. There are numerous lists of selfish listening habits. Consider the following most often listed behaviors:

1. **Interrupting**
2. **Switching the topic**
3. **Avoiding eye contact**
4. **Being distracted by something around the conversation**

5. **Making a response that is totally unrelated to what the other person has just talked about**
6. **Think about what to say next while others are still talking**
7. **Finishing the other person's sentences**
8. **Not showing much interest in what the other person is talking about**
9. **Showing impatience**
10. **Giving the impression that you're really just waiting for the person to finish so that you can talk**
11. **Biases and prejudices**

And the list could go on and on. You could eliminate many of these and other listening problems if you just focused on the other person more than on yourself. When you're self-involved and uncaring about the other person and what they have to say, you aren't listening at any level. You'll never create common ground connections either because you won't be able to collect the information necessary about the other person that will help you do that. You won't be communicating in a way that builds a relationship with others either.

Taken a step further, self-centered listening behaviors can be downright annoying. You may irritate others because you're discounting them and what they have to say. That irritation becomes a distraction for them in the conversation.

What's important is not generic lists of selfish listening behaviors, but identifying the poor listening behaviors you typically use in talking with others. Once identified you can then work on changing those behaviors.

Realize that focusing on the other person is not complete selflessness. You'll still get what you need from a given conversation. All that you're doing when you focus on the other person is saying: "You go first."

6. Actions of listening

It would seem like explaining the process by which you listen would be easy and straightforward. We all listen. Sometimes, we don't listen very well, but most of the time we're pretty good at it. But there's a lot more to it. Authors and researchers have attempted for over 30 years to explain the process of listening with very little consensus.

The following three actions are an attempt to create a short list of the listening process: (1) receiving information/paying attention, (2) processing/understanding/interpreting, and (3) remembering.

Listening is a process which doesn't unfold in a linear, step-by-step fashion with a defined start and finish. Listening is a fast, complex process, with many overlapping components. The actions of listening go on simultaneously and with incredible speed in your conscious and unconscious mind. For example, in considering the previous three steps, you don't move from receiving information/ paying attention exactly down the list to remembering in any given conversation.

You use the parts of the process as you need them. When you're processing information, you might also be remembering a similar experience you had in the past. You might respond initially in a conversation, but then go back to receiving information/paying attention (Gerber & Murphy, 2020). You use these listening actions as needed to give you the best chance of listening effectively.

Receiving information/paying attention—attend/select/choose

All authors defining listening have as their first action the need for the person to "pay attention." You have hundreds of things vying for your attention in addition to listening to the other person with whom you're speaking. You must consciously attend/select/choose to what you will pay attention to. There are many factors that you use to make that determination such as follows:

1. **Are you interested in the subject being discussed?**
2. **Do you agree with what the person is sharing?**
3. **Do you like the person with whom you're talking?**
4. **What is your current physical state—are you tired, hungry, etc.?**

When you attend/select/choose some information, you also ignore or disregard other information. You need to choose the best information that will make your communication effective as well as make good decisions about what to ignore.

Processing/understanding/interpreting

What do you do with all the information you collect in paying attention? Most authors list the next action as understanding and interpreting that information from your own perspective.

You evaluate the information you see and hear for credibility and completeness. Is what the other person saying correct in your opinion? You may want to "read between the lines" if you feel the other person isn't being completely honest. It's important at this stage that both communicators also provide honest feedback to each other to make sure there is mutual understanding.

Remembering

Our conversations routinely involve remembering past experiences we've had that relate to the present conversation. How do you use your memory in conversations? There are many conceptualizations of how memory and listening work together, but much of the research indicates that your memory is characterized by the following two actions:

Short-term memory

Your short-term memory is a temporary storehouse of information which you use in your immediate conversations. It's about 30–45 seconds in length. Information in short-term memory is used immediately, passes into long-term memory, or is forgotten.

Long-term memory

Long-term memory is basically the permanent storehouse of all information you've ever experienced. It's unclear whether we "forget" things or just can't retrieve them from our memories. Many researchers believe that you never really forget anything. They point to evidence of someone suddenly remembering something they thought they had long since forgotten.

This phenomenon is called a "memory trace." This occurs when a memory is reactivated by something you're experiencing now. Each of us has had the experience of something you thought you had long forgotten coming back to your conscious thinking. Maybe there was a "trigger" event that reminded you of that forgotten information. Maybe it just popped into your head seemingly out of nowhere.

What do you remember from a given conversation and what do you forget? It really depends on a number of factors. If the person shared shocking information, you were probably more likely to remember. If you weren't really interested in the story they shared, you probably won't remember.

Your motivation to remember may be the most important factor in remembering. For example, let's say that you are taking a college class in interpersonal communication. You know a friend of yours took the same class with the same instructor last semester. The next time you see them, you ask them about their experience in that class. When they share their lessons learned from that class, you're likely to listen intently to what they're saying because it's very relevant to you. In this case, you'll make a greater effort to remember what they share because you probably want a good grade. The number of factors which you use to determine what you want to remember is endless and really specific to the people and the conversation.

What's important is that you don't remember all that's said to you. You just forget some things. Studies have shown that most people only remember about 25% of what they listen to. This is just the reality of human information processing. At some point in the conversation, you must make a decision about what you want to "try" to remember and what you need to just let go. That decision is up to you.

Think of the last time you had a conversation with someone. After leaving that conversation, you probably remember some of what was shared but not all of it. You probably remembered at least the general idea of what you talked about but not every specific detail. Given the number of conversations you have every day with lots of different people, it's probably best that you can't remember everything. Without some forgetting, you'd be overloaded.

Most people don't really think about the possibility that they can impact their listening through their memories. They just access their memories in conversations without too much thought and hope for the best. But, by being more aware of your memory, you may be better able to control and direct a mental process that is integral to effective listening and ultimately creating common ground connections.

7. Changing the world one person at a time

How can we really make a difference in our respective lives and in the world? One of the most important actions we can take is simply to listen to one another. As stated at the beginning of this chapter, listening is a gift we give to every person with whom we talk. Each of us has a tremendous capacity to listen to others. It's amazing how much we connect with another human being by simply listening to them.

Specifically, what does that mean? As detailed in this chapter, build on your existing skills. Use them as a basis for understanding others. But be willing to modify those skills, use them differently, or even learn new skills. Integrate your listening skills into the common ground connections approach to help you listen better than you ever have.

When you consider the divisiveness currently in the United States, and the world, we need to step up our efforts to listen to everyone regardless of their perspective. When we talk with people who have different beliefs, "hear them out." Give them a chance to fully explain their viewpoint.

This is not easy to do when you communicate with a person who represents a group you find reprehensible. In no way does this person have a perspective that you would ever consider acceptable. But we begin to reduce the divisiveness in the country by doing just that—listening. Listening and processing what the other person says is the only real way we can begin to find common ground and possibly a connection.

The United States has always been a diverse country characterized by dissent. But that's what's made the country strong. Without dissent we'd be a country where women and young people couldn't vote, minorities would have no rights, members of the LGBTQ+ community could not marry in any state, and workers wouldn't have protections. Currently, dissent in the United States may have gone too far. Can we heal our country?

The sentiment of healing a divided America has started to happen on a person-to-person, grassroots level. One example is a non-profit non-partisan umbrella group called the Bridge Alliance. The Bridge Alliance consists of over 70 cross-partisan groups from towns throughout the country with 3 million supporters. These groups sprang up locally in an effort to restore respect and explore points of agreement with diverse individuals and groups in their respective communities (Hochschild, 2018).

The Bridge Alliance and other similar groups demonstrate that Americans realize there's a problem. These groups have all taken the first step in fixing that problem . . . listening to one another. That includes people we find offensive, who make us angry, and with whom we believe we have nothing in common.

When we start listening to people more we begin to create common ground connections with others like we never thought possible. This means that we get closer to people with whom we already agree like our immediate circle of family and friends, our communities, and work colleagues. But we also begin to connect with people with whom we disagree not only in our personal lives but also within the country.

Imagine what the world would be like if everyone made more of an effort to really listen to one another. We could put our differences on hold while we explored viewpoints different from our own. We could begin to understand different perspectives without hating people who hold those perspectives. Creating common ground connections would become the norm for everyone because everyone was using their listening skills to the fullest.

Bibliography

Chartrand, T. L., & Bargh, J. A. (1999). The chameleon effect: The perception-behavior link and social interaction. *Journal of Personality and Social Psychology*, 76(6), 893–910.

Collins, D. (2022, July 23). We are in COVID denial. *The Day*.

Fagan, M., & Huang, C. (2019, April 18). A look at how people around the world view climate change. *Pew Research Center*.

Fatherree, D. (2022, March 11). Pushing back hate: The year in hate and extremism 2021 examines how communities work for justice. *Southern Poverty Law Center*.

Florida, R. (2018, March 15). Where hate groups are concentrated in the U.S. *Bloomberg*.

Gerber, P. J., & Murphy, H. (2020). I.C.A.T. Interpersonal Communication Abridged Textbook. *CNM (Central New Mexico Community College)*.

Hipona, G. (2020, October 13). Social media and active listening skills don't seem to mix. *Counseling Today*.

Hochschild, A. R. (2018, January 19). Trump has divided the country. Some Americans are trying to bring us back together. *Time*.

Lopez, D. (2022, May 12). Poll finds one-third of adults say they think an effort is afoot to replace native-born Americans with new immigrants for electoral purposes. *AP*.

Maslin, M. (2019, November 28). The five corrupt pillars of climate change denial. *The Conversation*.

Nichols, R. G., & Stevens, L. A. (1957). Listening to people. *Harvard Business Review*, 2019 reprint.

Schwartz, J. M., & Begley, S. (2002). *The mind and the brain: Neuroplasticity and the power of mental force*. Regan Books/Harper Collins Publishers.

Tan, S. (2016, June 20). How well do you handle change? The benefits of being adaptable. *Business.com*.

Valko, L. (2022, March 2). Why HSPs tend to be exceptional listeners. *Highly Sensitive Refuge*.

7

SHARED PERCEPTIONS

The nature of perception

Perception helps you understand how you experience the world around you. You pick up what you perceive primarily through your five senses: touch, sight, sound, smell, and taste (Cherry, 2022). You process that information through various cognitive processes. This process never stops.

We all possess an infinite number of perceived experiences that are unique to each of us and no one else (Shaw, 2015). Those experiences are what define us. They include our likes and dislikes, attitudes, values, beliefs, and other aspects of who we are (Ahmed, 2019).

When we switch to try to understand the perceptions of others, we can become derailed. Consider just these different perspectives in a "typical" conversation that can sometimes keep us from understanding others:

- What I actually thought I said to you.
- What the other person actually heard (according to them).

DOI:10.4324/9781003357049-7

- What the other person thought they said to me.
- What I actually heard (according to me).
- The mental processing unique to me in interpreting what's going on.
- The mental processing that is going on with the other person.

This means that two people can potentially perceive the same things very differently. For example, two people can perceive the same political candidate in completely different ways despite having the same exposure to that candidate. Those two people may have heard the same speeches, ads, and television appearances from the candidate, but each is still perceiving the candidate differently. This is because whatever each person is seeing and hearing is passing through their unique perceptual frameworks which includes biases and prejudices.

Is perception reality?

Each person constructs their own version of the people and events in their life. Many researchers believe that there is no "objective" reality shared by everyone. You use your perceptions to re-construct what is reality for you. Then you use that constructed reality to communicate with everyone else who has constructed their own reality as well.

The perceptions of those two people will never be completely the same. We can try to get close, however, by "sharing" perceptions. The goal is to use the common ground connections approach to more easily and accurately develop a common reality that both conversational partners share and understand.

Shared perceptions in the world

Are we currently sharing perceptions in the world? It doesn't appear so. Eight in 10 Americans and 7 in 10 people globally (BBC World Survey, 2018) believe the people in their countries have a range of diverse perspectives. But is this perception completely accurate?

A "perception gap"

Viewpoint #1: the perception gap is real

The difference between public perceptions and reality on a wide range of issues is called the "perception gap." A study by the group "More in Common" of 2,100 Americans on a range of issues showed the reality of the "perception gap" (More in Common, 2019). For example, in this survey, this research group discovered that Democrats and Republicans significantly overestimate by almost double how many of the members of the other party hold "extreme views" on issues (Stevens,

2019). Consider other examples of the perception gap in the world from Duffy (2022):

1. Six in 10 people across 40 countries think that vaccines and autism are linked. Evidence with over 1 million children indicates that's not true.
2. Across 30 countries, only 15% of people think their national murder rate is down since 2000. In reality, the murder rate is down drastically.
3. French people currently believe 30% of their population are Muslim. The actual number is around 8%.

These and other misperceptions are perpetuated by politicians, the media, and social media. We often want simple answers to complex problems, but that's often not reality.

Viewpoint #2: the perception gap is overstated

Some research has shown that the majority of people in the world hold perceptions that are often very similar. Yet over time, people have increasingly developed a distorted understanding of each other. This calls into question this "perception gap" idea.

Americans are less divided than many believe. The majority of people comprise an "exhausted majority" who hold more moderate views on a range of issues. This moderate majority is frustrated with a world that is dominated by people on the extremes who seem to dominate the media (Stevens, 2019).

What might help each of us to realize is that the view of the world as divided is really a perception of the situation. It's an interpretation or opinion about how we view people and the country as a whole. Perceptions can often be accurate or have at least some truth to them, but sometimes that just isn't the case. Perceptions can be wrong.

Preview of chapter

This chapter attempts to untangle the complexity of perception in communication situations. Perception enables you to collect the information you need to communicate effectively with each person. The accuracy of those perceptions determines how successful you are in creating common ground connections.

1. Common ground connections and perception
2. How common ground connections support your perceptual accuracy
3. Common ground connections and perceptual patience
4. Personal factors that impact how you perceive others
5. Your mind and perception
6. Concepts of perception

7. Actions of the perceptual process
8. We need to talk more about what unites us

1. Common ground connections and perception

(1) **Focus on the other person:** Focusing on the other person is essential in developing accurate perceptions of others. Accurate perceptions are only possible when we understand "where the person's coming from." This isn't always easy because everyone can approach a situation from a slightly different angle.

In emphasizing a focus on the other person, you can more easily see that what might be an obvious interpretation for you might not be so obvious to the other person (Rogers, 2017). By focusing on the other person you're collecting more information than you might normally about how the other person views something.

(2) **Establish common ground:** When you seek to establish common ground you're trying to "share" perceptions. You want to know how the other person sees an issue. You compare that with your own perception of that issue. Two people often realize that their common ground is really a shared perception.

(3) **Connect with others:** In order to "connect" with others you have to thoroughly explore the perspective of another person on a given issue. If you discover a shared perspective, you begin to work on a connection with them.

(4) **Take advantage of your current communication skills:** You have a lifetime of experience in successfully interacting with others who possess many different perspectives on a number of issues. Try the skills you've had success with before within the context of the common ground connection approach to achieve the best outcomes.

2. How common ground connections support your perceptual accuracy

There are three ways in which common ground connections can help give you the information you need to be accurate in your perceptions of others.

(1) **Clarifying the perceptions of others:** Common ground connections helps you clarify your perceptions of others by giving you more information than you may be used to. You take all the information you've gathered and determine the points on which you can create common ground and potentially a connection.

(2) **Clarifying your own perceptions:** Common ground connections help you to understand your own perceptions as well. Particularly

in conflict situations, you need to understand how your perspective is being understood by the other person. Are you making yourself clear for example? Are you saying something that's offensive to them? With common ground connections you're sharing information back and forth with another person as you seek commonalities.

(3) **Building relationships:** Relationships are built when two people begin to really understand one another. With common ground connections you simply get to know each other better. When you get to know someone on a more personal level as you do with this approach, you understand them better.

The previous points are actions that can be taken at any point in a conversation to work on understanding a diverse range of perspectives. Use them as needed based on what you believe you need as the conversation progresses.

3. Common ground connections and perceptual patience

One of the unique aspects of creating common ground connections through the perceptions you adopt is the importance of patience in interpreting what the other person is communicating. You can't always be in a rush or jump to conclusions based on what someone says at a given point in time. People say all kinds of things. What they say may not really be what they mean. The common ground connections approach encourages an ongoing level of patience. The reason is you must continue to focus on the other person and build an understanding of their perspective over the life of a conversation.

It often takes time to really understand what the other person is communicating. For example, I may conclude from what the other person initially says in a conversation at work that they really hate their current boss. They perceive their boss as verbally abusive and disagreeable. But as the conversation progresses, I conclude that they don't really "hate" their boss as much as they communicated. My initial perception was clouded by the person's emotions when they first started sharing with me. They were apparently just "blowing off steam" from a recent conversation. They may in fact like their boss most of the time. Apparently, the day before the boss criticized a project on which the person had worked. Your friend thought the criticism was unfair.

Demonstrating patience in communication is particularly important in conversations in which you're having conflict with a person. I may have trouble understanding your opinion on an issue because I think it's so different from mine. But, if I'm patient I collect more information from which I can begin to understand your viewpoint better.

4. Personal factors that impact how you perceive others

There are four personal factors which are common to all of us that impact our perceptions. These are a natural part of each person's information processing that can sometimes help and sometimes hinder your ability to perceive the world and others accurately. The four factors are as follows:

(1) **Demographic factors:** Demographic factors like your age, sexual orientation, marital status, amount of education, profession, gender and physical characteristics can impact how you perceive things. If you're 70 years old, you're going to perceive cell phones as curious, but not necessarily something you use very often if at all. You didn't grow up with cell phones and don't necessarily see the necessity of being in constant contact with everyone.

In contrast if I'm an 18-year old college student, I may be obsessed with my cell phone checking it constantly and making it the center of my life. I use it in every part of my life including in the car and in classes. The 70-year old doesn't understand this cell phone obsession. The 18-year old perceives their actions as just a natural part of life.

Demographic factors make up who you are as a unique individual. These factors make communication with others interesting, but can also present challenges to understanding if you fail to consider them in conversations.

(2) **Your past experiences:** The influence of past experiences can include anything from your childhood to something you did last week. Each person has an unlimited number of past experiences from which to draw. All these experiences are unique to you.

Even brothers and sisters in the same family may possess different perspectives of the same family experiences. You might remember the camping trip you went on with your family when you were 11 as great. You got to camp out, grill hot dogs on an open fire, and even see a live bear. Your sister who was 16 at the time didn't share you perception of the trip. She particularly didn't like the fact that she wasn't able to shower for 3 days.

(3) **Your culture:** The culture in which you were raised also shapes your opinions, beliefs, values and thus your perceptions. Often you react to others based on how your family and friends reacted as you were growing up. Plus, all of us have had our own unique "cultural" experiences. For example misunderstandings can result when you try to peg people into a specific culture based on the label you assign them. Let's say you have a friend who has identified herself as "Hispanic." What does that mean really? Did her family grow up in Mexico, and then immigrated to the United States? Did their family raise them like other parents in America do? Did they continue the cultural practices inherent to how someone in Mexico might live? Did they observe typical American holidays and observances?

The point is there isn't just one kind of Hispanic person in the United States. Each Hispanic person is unique. If you're going to create common ground connections with your Hispanic friend, you must determine how she defines her culture. If you fail to do this, then you're trying to relate to her using faulty perceptions.

(4) **Your present feelings:** Perception can be affected by your thoughts and feelings as a conversation progresses. If you're tired and irritable, you're going to communicate differently than if you're rested and refreshed. If you're hungry, you're probably going to be easily distracted from a conversation by your hunger pangs and the donuts in the break room.

5. Your mind and perception

As covered in the chapter "The Unconscious Communicator," your brain is confronted by vastly more information from the world than you can process. All this would be chaos without the conscious and unconscious parts of your brain making sense of it by organizing it into patterns and categories (Lipari, 2015). These constructed patterns and categories are your perceptions. They enable you to make interpretations of people and events based on your past experiences, beliefs, values, and what's happening in the current conversation. These are obviously different from person to person.

(1) **Your conscious mind and perception:** Consciously, your brain helps you to construct the perceptions you need in the moment. Your conscious mind is using all the resources it has to try to make sense of what's going on. Sometimes what you construct consciously can be very accurate. Sometimes it isn't. For example you often perceive what you expect to see which may or may not be accurate without giving it too much thought.

(2) **Your unconscious mind and perception:** The vast majority of your perceptions are unconscious and done out of habit (Lipari, 2015). There are times when you realize consciously that you're using information from your unconscious to interpret conversations and understand others. That isn't always the case however.

There are other times when your unconscious can impact your current perceptions without you even being aware of it. For example, you might not even realize you're judging someone because of their race. You don't realize what you're doing, but they do. If you unconsciously communicate in a condescending way with a Black man because you don't consider him your equal, you may make subtle racist comments for example. Because it isn't good to be a racist in society, you've pushed your racist opinions to your unconscious, but they surface often unknowingly. The Black man with whom you're talking definitely notices.

6. Concepts of perception

The following concepts are really how each of us "perceives" our environment. If you can learn to be aware of these conscious and unconscious processes, you'll develop more accurate perceptions.

(1) **Thin slices:** occur when you make judgments about the communication behavior of others based on quick, initial observations of their verbal and nonverbal behavior. Do you remember a time when you met someone and immediately formed a negative impression of them? Maybe they seemed very aggressive in talking and tried to intimidate you by standing too close during the conversation. As you got to know them, however, your initial negative impression of the person changed. You came to accept that the person's aggressiveness was just how they communicated. It wasn't really directed at you personally. You actually became very good friends with them. Thin slices can work the other way too. You were at a friend's party and met someone to whom you were initially attracted. They were physically attractive, outgoing, and seemed to have a contagious charisma. Your initial perception of them or thin slice was very positive. You were looking forward to a possible long-term relationship. After going on one date with them however, you were able to peel the onion on this person to uncover some very selfish and aggressive qualities. Your initial thin slice of the person became more informed and changed significantly—in this case negatively. Thin slicing is a natural part of how we perceive others. Research has shown that thin slices can be surprisingly accurate at times (Ambady et al., 2000; Ambady and Rosenthal (1992). But, they can also be wrong. There are times when you need more information than thin slices can provide if you're going to communicate with understanding.

• **The stubbornness of "thin slices":** The other problem with "thin slicing" is that once you've created a thin slice of someone you tend to hold on to it. This is often true even when later you perceive contradictory evidence from the other person that disproves your initial perception. You can't help forming thin slices of others. But, to communicate effectively you need to be willing to change them as needed. We're always going to use "thin slices" when we communicate with others. But, when we seek common ground connections we must learn to go beyond.

(2) **We fill-in:** You fill-in gaps in what you pick up from another person according to your own experiences and frames of reference. Someone you meet for the first time might appear to be very quiet and shy. You don't really know that, but you assume that they are because they don't talk much as the conversation progresses. You form an initial opinion of the person and fill-in a whole bunch of other characteristics on your own.

You fill-in because you're driven to "make sense" of a situation. This is a reasonable process given what you have to work with. The problem is that often these first impressions can inaccurate. As you get to know this person, you discover the quiet and shy person inn the sample above isn't actually very outgoing. In other words, filling in is fine as long as you don't fill-in with concrete and stay open to learning more about a conversational partner.

(3) **We reconstruct what we perceive:** We reconstruct what we perceive to make sense of it. Sometimes our reconstructions aren't an accurate picture of the other person or the conversation (Cytowic, 2017). Also, two people can reconstruct a situation or subject very differently.

(4) **False consensus effect:** This effect occurs because you overestimate the extent to which other people are like you in terms of viewpoints, preferences, and values. It's a cognitive bias that leads people to believe that their viewpoints are "normal" and shared by most people.

Are there times when you're more likely to be guilty of the false consensus effect? Consider these factors:

- **Importance:** If you believe that a particular perspective or point of view you hold is really important, you're more likely to hang on to that belief. In reality the importance of an issue for you may not have anything to do with whether others feel the same way.
- **Confidence:** If you are 100% confident in your point of view you're more likely to assume most people agree with you. Your level of confidence may make you a good debater on an issue, but it doesn't mean anyone necessarily agrees with you.

(5) **Stereotyping:**

Stereotypes are generalizations about groups that are applied to the individuals who are members of that group. Stereotyping is when you believe in oversimplified assumptions about someone that are: 1) not based on factual knowledge, and 2) based on only a few experiences. These assumptions do not justify making a generalization about that person (Monnet, 2018).

There are stereotypes about every person in the world including males and females, Blacks, Italians, Hispanics, and every other race and nationality. Although there are positive stereotypes, most stereotypes discriminate.

Problems occur when a stereotype of someone becomes so ingrained in our minds, that it becomes resistant to change. Stereotypes ignore the basic principle of human communication: we're all individuals with our own unique characteristics.

(6) **Confirmation bias:** Confirmation bias occurs when you favor information that confirms your previously held beliefs or biases. Confirmation bias impacts how you gather information, but also how you interpret that information. If I'm pro-abortion rights, I will tend to seek out news that supports my existing ideas. I will tend to ignore any information that challenges my opinion. I'm not likely to read an article online about the Roe vs. Wade, 2022 decision by the Supreme Court. I would want to know more about the overwhelming vote in August, 2022 by the people in Kansas to keep abortion legal in that state (Lysen et al., 2022).

If you're going to create common ground connections, you have to stay aware of the tendency we all have of considering only information that supports our opinions and perspectives. When I'm guilty of confirmation bias, I prevent myself from getting all the information I need, positive and negative, on a situation or person. Even the common ground connections I establish may be inaccurate if I don't consider all information whether I agree with it or not.

(7) **Expectations:** We often perceive what we expect or want to perceive. Whether we are consciously aware of it, our expectations of someone will seep into our communications with them (Sexton, 2019).

For example, think about the last time you started a class with a professor you didn't know. Did you have any expectations at the outset that influenced how you actually experienced the class as the semester continued? If you heard that the professor was boring, were you more likely to be bored on the first day or on subsequent days?

(8) **Self-fulfilling prophecy:** You take the influence of your expectations to the next level when you engage in self-fulfilling prophecies. This means that when you expect people to act in a certain way your predictions will frequently come true. This is in part because you're only perceiving the information that confirms your beliefs. You act on perceptions as if they were true. You often "help" the person act in a manner which will fulfill your predictions (Ackerman, 2018).

The following is an example of how the self-fulfilling prophecy concept works:

• **Example: Political skew**

Step #1: You perceive a local politician in a certain way.

Example: You've heard very negative things about a local politician. You don't agree with her stance on any issue. You feel she's abandoned her local constituents by pandering to local big money interests in her district. You don't have any direct research or data that confirms your beliefs, but that's what you've come to believe.

Step #2: Going forward you act as if your perception of the candidate is true whether it's true or not. You don't necessarily seek more information to confirm or dis-confirm your perception.

Example: As the campaign for this politician's seat draws near you work diligently to block her re-election. You make speeches within the district to establish a very negative view of this politician's record. You have very little data on her voting record or bills passed, but what data you do collect is only the information that supports your position. You support the opposing candidate even going door-to-door. Your opinion of the politician and your efforts to unseat her increases the probability that your original perceptions will come true, and the other candidate will win.

Step #3: You observe the actions of the person for whom you have this negative perception. You internalize only the behaviors of the person that agree with your original perception. You ignore any behaviors of that person that may challenge your perspective.

Example: During the campaign you hear the politician speak at a political event. Your ongoing negative perception of this person leads you to notice only the negative qualities of her speech. You ignore the audience at the event which seems excited by the person including many instances when they enthusiastically applaud. Instead, you only form the opinion that the politician is a poor speaker and is unclear on her record.

7. Actions of the perceptual process

Three conceptualizations of the actions of the process of perception are the following: (1) selection, (2) organization, and (3) interpretation. There are often different labels used, but these are generally the actions that have the most research support.

These actions of the process of perception happen so quickly we're often not even aware of them. In any conversation, you're selecting, organizing, and interpreting non-stop. They're all completely entangled because that's how quickly your mind moves to keep up with any conversation. You use whatever actions you need at given points in a conversation to make sense of what the other person is saying. You don't go "lock step" through the actions.

The whole process of which these three actions are a part is already a natural process of your mind with which you are usually highly skilled. Sometimes, though you need a little help in untangling this process and becoming more aware of how this all works in an actual conversation. Some concepts included here were highlighted in "The Unconscious Communicator" chapter.

(1) Selection

Each of us has to pay attention, focus, and zero in on the tremendous amount of information with which we are confronted in every conversation. It's not possible for anyone to process everything. Using your mind you select what actions and information you want to deal with at any one time. This is how the process of perception starts (Lipari, 2015).

Your mind selects information from a conversation in a number of ways. Specifically, you filter the available information by using the three processes further explained in the listening chapter: 1) selective attention, 2) selective exposure, and 3) selective retention. Selective attention simply means that you choose to what you want to pay attention. You have to ignore some information.

Selective exposure is defined as the tendency for you to expose yourself to certain people and topics and to avoid other people and topics. If you're a liberal democrat, you may tend to avoid conservative republicans. You may not want to expose yourself to their beliefs with which you disagree.

Selective retention is the belief that you remember some things to which you've heard and seen, but forget others. You select what you'll retain based on personal preferences, what you need at the time to understand what's happening in a conversation, and other reasons that are personal and unique to you.

This process of selection is important in creating common ground connections because it can help you understand another person. Analyze your process of selection. Ask yourself: "Am I selecting the right information to best understand the person and their communication?" As you practice this increased awareness, you'll be able to build your skills in gathering the most important information you need.

(2) Organization

Another action of perception is organization. This is when you organize the information you perceive in some way. Each individual has a different way they categorize information in their mind depending on what they think they need to understand the other person. Once again it's related to past perceptions and experiences as well as the current situation.

• **Schemas**

One way you organize information from conversations is by creating schemas or using existing schemas. Schemas are like a script you've constructed in your mind that describe how another person typically communicates. It includes what they say, what they do, how you usually describe their communication, subtle meanings you usually pick up, and other aspects of their communication. Schemas allow you to interpret the communication of others without having to start over in every conversation.

You might think of schemas as a road map with specific instructions for navigating through the interpersonal world. That map has instructions, guidelines, suggestions, and even questions you use when interacting with each person in your life. You develop a schema or script of the communication characteristics for all of the people with whom you communicate. It's believed that each person has hundreds of schemas which are formed from the earliest part of life. They continue to form and change throughout your life.

You draw on your set of schemas to successfully navigate the conversation in which you find yourself at the time. Scarvalone et al. (2005) point to the adaptability of these schemas when in actual use:

Moreover, when new interpersonal encounters occur and a schema is triggered, experienced, and appraised, any new information becomes assimilated into the already existing structure (p. 365).

There are other times when if you don't have a schema for a particular person that makes sense in describing their communication you can form a new one. You mentally log their verbal and nonverbal communication behaviors into a temporary schema which you might change based on your future conversations with them.

Are we consciously aware of these schemas? Research to date indicates that sometimes we are and sometimes we're not. Baldwin and Dandeneau (2005) hypothesize that relationship schemas function automatically, producing their effects quickly (e.g., within a fraction of a second) and even outside awareness (p. 319). At other times, however, schemas seem to be very much controlled by us.

Schemas are an important mental tool in helping you understand the people with whom you already have a relationship. When you use schemas with someone you know, you generally have an advantage. You understand "how" they generally communicate. This will help you in understanding them in the present conversation.

More importantly, if the person isn't communicating in accordance with your schema, you may want to try to determine what's going on. It could be the person is just very emotional about a traumatic situation they're in. Or maybe the person is deliberately hiding something from you because they're embarrassed. It doesn't mean you completely throw out your existing schema, just that you need to talk further to understand what's going on. You adjust your schema of this person as necessary.

If on the other hand, this is the first time you've interacted with a person, you'll still try to use schemas to understand them. In this case you compare schemas from similar people you know with this new person. Your schema of this new person continues to build as you talk with the individual. Eventually, you begin to develop a more substantial schema that is unique to this new person you've just met.

You don't want to over-rely on schemas. It's tempting once a schema is formed to continue to use it in every conversation. But, people can change and all conversations should be considered unique. If you use old schemas you won't have the flexibility to really understand a person in a particular conversation.

- **Conscious schemas**

  You're usually aware of the conscious schemas you use in your communication. For example I may realize that I don't like talking with people who talk too much. I believe that because I like to talk too. When someone talks to much, I never get a chance to share my ideas. If that schema operates in a given conversation in which I'm involved, I may try to interject my ideas or leave the situation completely. I will take note to avoid conversations with that person in the future.

- **Unconscious schemas**

  You also have developed schemas that are unconscious. You're not even aware that you have them. You might hold a prejudice against Hispanics for example that you might not even realize. You developed this schema years ago when you had some bad experiences with Hispanics at your high school. Despite the fact that your experiences since high school have been very good with that group, you've held onto that negative schema and use it in your current conversations.

  How do you know if you have an unconscious schema against Hispanics now? You may not know other than being aware of the negative ways Hispanics react to you and your communication. They'll know you have negative perception of them by what you say and do, but may not challenge you about those perceptions.

  Common ground connections also asks you to think about your communication and conversations much more actively than you may be used to. This means that you must put mental energy into what schemas may be operating in a conversation—your own and the other person with whom you're talking. Because you're so focused on the other person with this approach, you'll be able to pick up on how others are reacting to the schemas that you may be using.

- **Societal schemas**

We have seen and continue to see the operation of schemas between different groups in the United States. For example, people of the Jewish faith have always been discriminated against. Not just in Nazi Germany, but continuing through to today with recent synagogue shootings. Some people have negative conscious and unconscious "Jewish" schemas which are the basis for their hatred of Jews. They may realize they have an "anti-Jewish" schema, but not really understand why they hate Jewish people so much.

There are schemas against Blacks too. From slaveholders in the 1800s to today, Blacks are discriminated against because of the color of their skin. If someone sees a Black person in today's world, their schema of that person is often negative. Some people indicate that Black people are better off today than they were 50 years ago. The real question is: "Is that really true?" Some would say yes. Some would say it's just more of the same, but in a different wrapper.

If we want to be effective communicators who seek to understand every person, we need to stay aware of those times when our schemas are operating. Are we using negative schemas sometimes without thinking about it when we communicate with certain groups? If we find that we're using prejudicial and biased schemas, we need to have the flexibility to change those schemas.

(3) **Interpretation:** The final action of the perception process is interpretation. With this action, you assign meaning to the information you've selected and organized from a conversation. You then take the information you've perceived and turn it into something you can categorize and understand. Your interpretations are based on your experiences, needs, wants, values, expectations and a number of other factors important at the time of the conversation.

These actions of the process of perception: 1) selection, 2) organization, and 3) interpretation are already a natural process of your mind with which you are highly skilled. Sometimes though you need a little help in untangling this process and becoming more aware of how all this works.

8. We need to talk more about what unites us

The More in Common organization conducted a study called the Hidden Tribes Project that sought to determine the extent and accuracy of perceptions in the United States. Even though research shows that Americans often have more in common than they believe, the following misperceptions perpetuate our current divisions (Yudkin et al., 2019):

1. **Those with the greatest levels of hostility towards their political opponents typically understand them the least.** This could be used as a basis for a more productive and extensive dialogue between opposing groups.
2. **Whether intentionally or unintentionally, Americans increasingly live within isolated information bubbles.** What is needed are more common accepted sources of information from different media outlets.
3. **People with different perspectives overestimate the magnitude of the differences between them and the other side.** Often they don't really understand what the other side believes.

Can we identify steps we can use to address these misperceptions that are dividing us? This would reduce the "threat" both sides are feeling from their opponents, and start a more productive dialogue with everyone involved.

If we're going to move forward in the world, we need to pull everyone together regardless of their perspective to develop solutions to our problems everyone will support. We need to be able to accept that there will be differences in how issues are perceived and the approaches to solve those issues. Instead of emphasizing perspectives that divide us we need to talk about what we share and what unites us (Adamec & Kendall-Taylor, 2021).

We need to really take to heart the fact that "people often don't perceive things the way I do," and avoid getting angry when they don't. Then, we can seek to understand not only what others believe but also why they believe the way they do. At that point, the magic of common ground connections can happen.

Bibliography

Ackerman, C. E. (2018, May 1). Self-fulfilling prophecy in psychology. *Optimism and Mindset.*

Adamec, S., & Kendall-Taylor, N. (2021, January 20). Commentary: America is not as divided as you think. Yes, really. *WBUR/Cognoscenti.*

Ahmed, A. (2019, February 5). Types of perception in communication. *Bizfluent.*

Ambady, N., Bernieri, F. J., & Richeson, J. A. (2000). Toward a histology of social behavior: Judgmental accuracy from thin slices of the behavioral stream. In M. P. Zanna (Ed.), *Advances in experimental social psychology* (Vol. 32, pp. 201–271). Academic Press.

Ambady, N., & Rosenthal, R. (1992). Thin slices of expressive behavior as predictors of interpersonal consequences: A meta-analysis. *Psychological Bulletin, 111,* 256–274.

Baldwin, M. W., & Dandeneau, S. D. (2005). Understanding and modifying the relational schemas underlying insecurity. In M. W. Baldwin (Ed.), *Interpersonal cognition* (pp. 33–61). Guilford.

BBC world survey: A world divided. (2018). Ipsos MORI Social Research Institute.

Brown, R. A., Helmus, T. C., Ramchand, R., Palimaru, A. I., Weilant, S., Rhodes, A., & Hiatt, L. (2021). *Violent extremism in America*. Rand Corporation.

Cherry, K. (November 8, 2022). What is perception? *Verywell Mind*.

Cytowic, R. E. (2017, May 2). Reality lies beyond what we can perceive. Psychology Today, Common Commons.

Duffy, B. (2022, June 22). The perception gap. *Constructive Institute*.

Fahkry, T. (2018, March 14). This is how perception creates your reality. Mission.org.

Felber, T. (2002). Am I making myself clear? Secrets of the world's greatest communicators. Thomas Nelson, Inc.

Lipari, L. (2015, January). Cure ignorance—human perception: Making sense of the world, UTNE Reader. *Lisbeth* (Reprinted with permission from Listening, Thinking, Being: Toward an ethics of attunement. Penn State Press, 2014).

Lysen, D., Ziegler, L., & Mesa, B. (2022, August 3). Voters in Kansas decide to keep abortion legal in the state, rejecting an amendment. *NPR* (Live coverage: 2022 primaries).

Monnet, J. (2018, February 7). How stereotypes affect communication. *Blog, Building bridges: Indo-European Intercultural Dynamics*.

Ray, R. (2020, June 19). What does 'defund the police' mean and does it have merit? *Brookings*.

Rogers, J. (2017, December 6). Perception: How your mind plays tricks on you. *Huffington Post*.

Scarvalone, P., Fox, M., & Safran, J. D. (2005). Interpersonal schemas: Clinical theory, research, and implications. In M. W. Baldwin (Ed.), *Interpersonal cognition* (pp. 359–387). Guilford Press.

Schaeffer, K. (2020, March 4). Far more Americans see 'very strong' partisan conflicts now than in the last two presidential years. *Pew Research Center*.

Sexton, C. (2019, November 12). How expectations change our perception of reality. *Earth.com*.

Shaw, L. (2015, April 30). Understanding perception is key to communication. *Forbes*.

Stevens, S. (2019, June 28). The perception gap: How false impressions are pulling Americans apart. *Heterodox Blog*.

Tate, J., Jenkins, J., & Rich, S. (2022, August 16). 1057 people have been shot and killed by police in the last year. Fatal Force Report. *The Washington Post*.

Thompson, C. W. (2015, January 25). Fatal police shootings of unarmed Black people reveal troubling patterns. *NPR*.

Wijnberg, R. (2019, December 24). More divided than ever? The truth is we agree much more than we think we do. *The Correspondent*.

Yudkin, D., Hawkins, S., & Dixon, T. (2019, June). The perception gap: How false impressions are pulling Americans apart. Hidden Tribes Project. *More in Common*.

8

CREATING PERSONAL CHANGE

If the idea of creating common ground connections sounds like a good idea for you in enhancing your current communication, you may need some support in that change.

Even though you're using existing skills in creating common ground connections, you'll still need to use those skills differently and in some cases more than you're used to. The purpose of this chapter is to provide you with realistic and practical guidelines for doing that.

DOI:10.4324/9781003357049-8

The guidelines included here are not dictatorial or directive. They're not intended to tell you what to do. They can't be because everyone's communication and their communication style are slightly unique to them. Each person must use the information in this book and the assistance in this chapter to determine what "best works for them" in terms of using the common ground connection approach.

In other words, each person must learn to be adaptable in incorporating common ground connection skills into their current communication style. This isn't always easy. As indicated elsewhere in this book, we often communicate out of habit more than anything else. We settle on a set of communication skills we use in the majority of our conversations that seem to work for us. And why not? If something seems to work, why change it? The problem is that it may not be "working" for us as much as we think.

Other people's reactions

As you modify your communication through common ground connections, you may notice that your conversations change. You may not be able to exactly "put your finger on it," but you know the communication is better for you.

Conversely, the people with whom you talk may notice that your communication with them has changed. They may even ask you about it. Regardless, they probably will like the change in the "new you" because you're communicating better and focusing more on them in every conversation.

Where do you begin?

Where do you begin in changing how you communicate? An easy first step is to use the actions of the common ground connections approach in one conversation. See how it goes. Then try your new way of communicating in a number of conversations. Develop a common ground connections approach that works for you in your unique conversations.

Think of the major transitions in your life. Sometimes it resulted from one big and perhaps traumatic event. But most of the time lasting change happens with small steps. For example, anyone who's tried to quit smoking knows it's tough to stop "cold turkey." Trying to lose weight is tough too. You only succeed by making small, steady steps.

And as we create changes in our life we often revert back to a previous set of behaviors that may feel more comfortable. This is particularly true if in trying the common ground connections approach you experience a conversation that doesn't go so well. Changing your communication will have some ups and downs. Starting small or at least realistically will help with this. The reality is that most of the time your previous communication wasn't really more comfortable just more familiar.

The context of your personal communication change

Changing your communication to a common ground connection approach may be a challenge in our current society. There seems to be so much divisiveness and conflict. There are so many sides and people with whom we don't agree. But keep in mind that this approach is particularly geared to communicating with people with whom we don't agree. Why? Because with this approach you need to focus on the other person and try to understand their perspective. When you do this, differences of opinion won't seem so "different." Conflicts will be less volatile because you're starting the conversation with them and what they have to say. This helps to clarify positions—yours and theirs. You don't find yourself in the position of "arguing on the same side" either.

There may be some people in your circle of friends, family, and work colleagues with whom you've never been able to understand or get along with. Try the common ground connections approach with that uncle who seems abrasive and insulting, or a colleague with whom you don't get along. You may come to realize that these people aren't so unlikable.

Preview of chapter

This chapter provides you with realistic and usable guidelines for adapting the common ground connections approach to enhance your personal communication. If you want to change your communication, you must use your full mental faculties and put forth a sincere effort. This chapter includes the following:

1. *Assessments:* to help you track your success in communicating differently using the common ground connections approach.

   1. **Personal assessment of your current communication skills**
   2. **Your experiences establishing common ground**
   3. **Your experiences "connecting" with another person**
   4. **Your experiences creating "common ground connections" with others**
   5. **Your communication goals**

2. *Personal factors:* explains the impact of your personality on changing your communication.

   1. **The degree to which you are selfish/self-centered**
   2. **Your obliviousness**
   3. **Your ego**
   4. **Your desire to control**

3. *Personal change guidelines:*

   1. **Use skills that fit your personality**
   2. **Adapt the skills to your various relationships**
   3. **Be patient with yourself**
   4. **Determine your motivation**

1. Assessments

1. **Personal assessment of your current communication skills.** This section gives you the opportunity to assess your current communication skills. As indicated earlier most of the time we don't think much about our communication. We just "communicate." But, to change your communication you must first assess where you are now in terms of your communication ability. What are your strengths? On what do you believe you need to work? This is essential in creating common ground connections because this approach builds on the communication skills that currently work for you.

   How do you do this? First of all, think about your communication when you're engaged in conversations. You can assess how you're doing and still engage actively in the conversation. After the conversation you may want to write down your thinking and observations about the conversation you just had. How did you do in communicating with the other person? What might you do differently next time?

   Second, ask the people with whom you typically talk. Ask their opinion about your communication. It may seem a little uncomfortable at first, but people generally appreciate your openness and willingness to improve your communication when you interact with them. Keep a record of the feedback you receive from others. Your personal feedback and feedback from others will give you a tremendous amount of information with which to adapt your current communication and best utilize the common ground connections approach.

Personal assessment: charting your communication skills

Instructions: Think about your current communication. What are your strengths and weaknesses in communicating with others? For the next week, really think about how you communicate in three conversations while you're having those conversations.

After the conversation is over, write down what you think you did well and what you could have done better. These can be verbal or nonverbal behaviors.

At the end of the week, draw some conclusions about how you currently communicate including aspects you want to change and aspects you want to continue.

Consider the following communication areas in filling this out:

1. Verbal skills
2. Nonverbal skills

3. Demonstrate positive listening skills
4. Show empathy, sincerity, and honesty
5. Avoid negative communication behaviors—anger, blame, defensiveness
6. Give and be open to feedback
7. Pay attention
8. Show enthusiasm for the other person and the conversation
9. Establish common ground
10. Create connections with others
11. Others?

Conversations --person, date, general subject.	What you did well.	What you could have done better.
#1:		
#2:		
#3:		

Conclusions

1. On what do you want to work?

2. What do you want to keep doing?

2: Your experiences establishing "common ground"

Instructions: In order to transition to the common ground connections approach you need to start becoming more aware of those times in your current conversations when you just establish common ground. In this section record those times in which you established common ground—either by accident or deliberately. There are charts that enable you to track "2" separate conversations.

Definition review—finding common ground:

Finding common ground with others simply means that we find things we have in common with them. We share interests, ideas, and even personal information about ourselves. We find commonalities not just differences. When we talk with people with whom we disagree, finding common ground will help us start a more productive dialogue with those people.

You establish common ground with people all the time. When you meet someone for the first time, what do you usually do? Most of the time, you try to find commonalities you share. Establishing common ground doesn't just happen with people you're meeting for the first time either. You also establish common ground with people you know well like family, friends, and spouses. For example how many times have you been talking to a friend and found out something completely new about them? This is common ground too. Your feelings of common ground in other words can change over time.

Unfortunately, we often don't deliberately seek to find common ground with others. Often it just happens. Yet, we all realize that finding common ground will help us communicate better with other people and it just feels good. The charting in this section of the chapter is intended to increase the times when you deliberately and more frequently seek common ground.

3: Your experiences "connecting" with another person

Instructions: The next step in developing a common ground connections approach for yourself is to develop an awareness of those times in your current conversations when you moved beyond common ground to deeper connections with a person. There are charts that enable you to track "2" separate conversations.

Definition review—connecting with others:

Sometimes we go deeper than common ground and create a "connection" with someone. Connecting with others means that two people are almost thinking in the same ways.

Conversation #1:
Observing and recording: Choose two future conversations to chart instances when you established common ground with another person. Make a conscious effort to establish that common ground. In the "description" section of the chart below analyze whether you felt you did in fact establish common ground: what you did, what the other person did, and what just seemed to happen. On what things did you establish common ground with them?
Description:
Name of other person: _____ Your relationship with this person: _____ Date of conversation: _____ Place of conversation: _____ Why did you feel you established common ground in this conversation?
Conversation #1: Your conclusions

Conversation #2:
Description:
Name of other person: _____ Your relationship with this person: _____ Date of conversation: _____ Place of conversation: _____ Why did you feel you established common ground in this conversation?
Conversation #2: Your conclusions

It might be that you're talking to a person and suddenly get a real sensation that both of you have established a closeness, a high level of agreement, even a shared consciousness. You could literally finish each other's sentences. A conversation that is free from confusion or judgment is created because the two people are basically communicating as one. You might have thought: "We really clicked."

Connection doesn't always have to be some super close connection. You can connect with anyone including the grocery store checkout person, a salesperson in a department store, or someone standing in line at your favorite fast food restaurant. The connection you establish with that "stranger" is still a connection because you're communicating for that brief moment in a way that both people can understand and feel good about.

Conversation #1:
Observing and recording: Choose two future conversations to chart instances when you established a "connection" with another person. Make a conscious effort to establish real connections as defined previously.
In the "description" section of the chart below analyze whether you felt you did in fact create a connection: what you did, what the other person did, and what just seemed to happen.
Description:
Name of other person: _____
Your relationship with this person: _____
Date of conversation: _____
Place of conversation: _____
Why did you think you created a connection with the other person in this conversation?
Conversation #1: Your conclusions

Conversation #2:
Description:
Name of other person: _____
Your relationship with this person: _____
Date of conversation: _____
Place of conversation: _____
Why did you think you created a connection with the other person in this conversation?
Conversation #2: Your conclusions

4: Your experiences creating "common ground connections" with others

Instructions: Now it's time to combine your efforts in establishing common ground and creating connections into common ground connections.

Definition review—common ground connections:

When you combine common ground and connecting into the common ground connections approach, you will realize the combined advantages of common ground and connection. You may also experience new benefits from combining both concepts you may not have realized before.

In seeking common ground connections you'll have to be more aware of the other person, the conversation, and your own communication. Keep your new focus on common ground connections in the back of your mind especially in real time when you're having a conversation. You'll have to actively think about this new way of communicating in every conversation with every person and then adjust accordingly. You'll soon begin to "sense" when you're being successful.

In this section record those times in two of your future conversations when you felt you established a "common ground connection" with another person.

Conversation #1:
Observing and recording: Choose a future conversation in the "Description" section below. Seek to establish a "common ground connection" with another person.   Then indicate whether you felt you did in fact create a "common ground connection" with the person: what you did, what the other person did, and what just seemed to happen.
Description:
Name of other person: _____   Your relationship with this person: _____   Date of conversation: _____   Place of conversation: _____   Why did you think you established a common ground connection?

Conversation #1: Your conclusions

Conversation #2:
Description:
Name of other person: _____   Your relationship with this person: _____   Date of conversation: _____   Place of conversation: _____   Why did you think you established a common ground connection?

Conversation #2: Your conclusions

#5: Your communication goals. If your goal is to change your communication, you need to clearly articulate what you intend to do, how you intend to do it, and how you will determine success. You also must write it down in order to fully commit to it.

Use these charts to set and track your goals in developing and transitioning to a common ground connection communication approach.

Goal #1:
What specific actions will you take to accomplish this goal?
How will you know you've been successful?

Goal #2:
What actions will you take to accomplish this goal?
How will you know you've been successful?

2. Personal factors

There are a number of personal factors that are particularly important for each of us to consider when changing any part of our life. These factors are particularly important when changing your communication.

As you attempt to transition to the common ground connections approach, consider the following personal factors that will impact your ability to make that change. The extent to which you "manage" these personal challenges will impact the degree to which you are successful. The personal factors particularly important in communication are as follows:

1. **The degree to which you're selfish/self-centered**
2. **Your obliviousness to others**
3. **Your ego**
4. **Your desire to control**

> 1. **The degree to which you are selfish/self-centered.** Selfish/self-centered communication is the result of being primarily concerned with oneself. If you're selfish/self-centered, you focus on yourself not other people with whom you have conversations. It really means that you're concerned more with yourself than for other people including their communication and what they may be thinking or feeling. A selfish/self-centered person is not likely to be interested or responsive to others (Barth, March 29, 2014).
>
> How do you know whether you're being selfish/self-centered? First of all, you don't ask many questions. You talk most of the time. You talk about what you want to talk about. If the other person tries changing the subject you bring the conversation back to what you want to talk about or to you.
>
> Second, you don't really listen to the other person. If someone asks you: "What do you think about what I just said?" You don't have a clue. You're engrossed in your own thoughts.
>
> Finally, if there's conflict, the selfish/self-centered person believes it's the other person's fault—not theirs. They take little responsibility for clear, mutual communication. The self-centered person's thinking is: "I communicated clearly. You just didn't understand it."
>
> Being selfish/self-centered flies in the face of one of the basics of creating common ground connections—focusing on the other person. The next time you're in a conversation monitor the amount of time you're focused on yourself versus the other person. If you find that most of the time you're focused only on yourself, try changing your focus. See what impact this will have on your ability to create common ground connections.

2. **Your obliviousness.** Sometimes we're not even aware that we're being selfish/self-centered. This is called obliviousness. Obliviousness is not "paying attention." But, it's more than that. Obliviousness is the tendency to be aware of only your own reality. You're basically unaware of the other person and what they're saying or feeling. You're focusing and concentrating on what you want to say not on the other person and what they're communicating.

This isn't effective communication. People don't like communicating with a person who is completely oblivious to them and what they have to contribute. The person who's the victim gets the feeling that they don't really need to be there. It's a one-sided speech for which the person didn't sign up. Oblivious communicators forget a basic factor in any conversation: "Communication is an interaction between two or more people who share a common understanding of information."

People don't mean to be oblivious, but they often get so wrapped up in their own concerns that they become oblivious to others and the world around them. Examples of oblivious communication are all around us. The individual who goes on and on talking without getting any input from you or asking for a response from you. The person who appears to be listening, but when a break comes in the conversation they start talking about a subject totally unrelated to what both of you were just talking about. Or the person you have conflict with because they can't or won't attempt to see your perspective. They only understand their own point of view. They're being deliberately oblivious because they don't want to hear any opinions that might question their point of view.

When you are oblivious you isolate yourself. The more you operate from only your own perspective the more limited your life becomes. Becoming more aware of your own obliviousness opens up your life and makes your life more meaningful through shared experiences. Sharing experiences with other makes it much easier to create common ground connections too.

3. **Your ego.** Everyone has an ego—the view they have of themselves. Simply, it's what you believe about yourself as a person.

Unfortunately, people's egos often become inflated and out of proportion to what might be a healthy self-concept. People with big egos believe they are a pretty fantastic person. As their ego grows their opinion of everyone else goes down. They may begin to believe that they have all the answers, and that other people therefore don't have much to offer.

People who have big egos will sometimes feel threatened for example if someone challenges their ideas in a conversation. The egotistical person may think: "I know more about this topic than anyone. How dare they challenge my opinion." With egotistical people you have to fight to be heard and for your opinions to be respected.

To realize the benefits of common ground connections you have to keep your ego in check. With your focus on the other person, you can't really be egotistical. Value yourself, but also realize those times when other people have the right to be heard. Be open to being influenced by other people and their perspectives.

4. **Your desire to control.** Ever have the feeling the people with whom you're interacting are choreographing the conversation? That is, they're controlling the direction of the conversation including the topics discussed and when you can talk? For example does the other person interrupt you when you're talking? Interrupting another person is a controlling response. It says that the other person isn't really listening to you.

An important part of the common ground connection approach is the importance of letting people be who they are. It includes letting the other person talk in full, and really listening to them.

Control as they say is an illusion anyway. You can't control another person and what they have to say. They're going to say what they want to say. That's not bad, it's interesting. People are unpredictable to a large extent. You're unpredictable. That's what makes human communication so interesting.

3. Personal change guidelines

If you want to use the information in this chapter to better create common ground connections, keep in the mind the following four points about personal change: (1) use skills that fit your personality, (2) adapt the skills to your current communication situations, (3) be patient with yourself, and (4) determine your motivation.

1. **Use skills that fit your personality.** Be realistic as to what you can do. Start slow. Stay within your comfort level. If you don't, any bad experiences may create a tendency not to try that skill again.
2. **Adapt the skills to your various relationships.** These skills must be used within the context of all your different relationships. Just like people, relationships vary on a number of dimensions. Use the skills you know from past experiences that will "fit" with the type of relationship in which you're trying the new skills. You might even want to share with your partner what you're doing.
3. **Be patient with yourself.** Using new communication skills or skills you already possess differently can often be difficult. Monitor what works. Keep trying, adjust, and you'll soon realize success.

4. **Determine your motivation.** Changing your current communication will require that you find the motivation to do so. It's just too easy to keep communicating the way you always have. Find a reason to change. If you're willing to do this, you'll realize specific advantages you may not have realized before. At a basic level you'll have more information and more accurate information to help you in understanding the other person and yourself.

Conclusion

This chapter has been about you and your desire to change your communication. When you change anything in your life, you'll have the most success when you make the changes gradually. This is how change "sticks" over the long haul. The charts in this chapter will hopefully help with that effort.

Bibliography

Ambler, C. (2015, September 14). Communicate without ego. *Daily Zen*.

Barth, F. D. (2014, March 29). 4 ways to deal with selfish people in your life. They know what they want. Do you? Off the couch. *Psychology Today*.

9

HEALING DIVISIVENESS

Communication for a divided world: common ground connections

The common ground connections approach to communication requires only a change in emphasis in your communication with others. You already possess these skills—you use them on a regular basis. But sometimes we don't use them even though we know the communication is clearer, results in greater under-standing, and just "feels good." The goal of the common ground connections

DOI:10.4324/9781003357049-9

approach is to use these natural skills in every conversation with every person with whom you interact.

Keep in mind the basics of success in using the common ground connections approach covered in Chapter 1:

1. **Always have as your primary goal in communicating with others to seek understanding.** That means doing your best to try to understand the other person and their perspective regardless of whether you agree with them or not.

2. **Keep your mind active and focused in every conversation with each person.** Use the almost unlimited power of your mind to manage your own thinking during conversations and process what the other person is sharing. For example catch yourself when you have a negative emotional response to what another person is saying. Deal with that thinking in order to avoid letting that emotion cloud your thinking.

3. **Make your first priority in every conversation the establishment of as much common ground as possible with that person.** This is obviously important when meeting someone for the first time or someone you don't know well. But, it's also true for people you know. When you continue to seek common ground in your ongoing relationships, you strengthen your bond with those people.

4. **Continually seek to use the aspects of common ground to develop connections throughout a conversation.** Use the aspects of the common ground you established with others to create deeper connections.

5. **Continue to use your best existing communication skills.** Build on your existing communication skills that already work for you. Integrate those skills into your common ground connections approach. Be flexible and adaptable so that you can best create an enhanced communication style that works for you in your unique conversations.

Dealing with "difficult" people

Will common ground connections work in the following "difficult" situations? Are some people so different from us that there's no way to create a common ground connection? Consider the following people:

- People with whom we have little or nothing in common
- People who hold angry and destructive opinions
- People who are apparently willing to do anything including the use of violence to make sure their perspectives are adopted

- People who seem inflexible and unwilling to see any perspective other than their own
- People who have no sense of loyalty to their "community"
- People who don't have a sense of their role in the world

Suggestions for "difficult" people and situations

1. **First, make sure you completely understand the other person's point of view.** Even if that person supports the use of violence and the elimination of personal liberties, you first must understand the details of their perspective. Why do this?

    - You can't refute an opinion of another person if you don't understand that opinion.
    - To deal effectively with such a situation you also have to compare your perspective to the other person's perspective. This comparison helps you to formulate arguments that you can utilize and that the other person may want to listen to.

2. **Second, make sure you clearly understand your own point of view and supporting evidence.** If you're challenged by the other person, you want to make sure that you're crystal clear on your ideas.

3. **Plan a strategy for having a conversation with this "difficult" person.** Think about how that person might respond to your main arguments in support of your perspective. "If you say this, what might they say" for example. Difficult conversations are made more difficult if you don't plan for the unexpected.

4. **Keep the main tenets of common ground connections in the back of your mind.** In particular, maintain a focus on the other person throughout the conversation. Avoid mentally developing counterarguments before thoroughly trying to understand the other person's perspective.

5. **Keep your emotions in check.** As indicated elsewhere in this book, sometimes people with whom we disagree say things that are offensive and completely out of step with anything we believe. When this happens, we get what some call an "anxiety spike." This occurs when we hear something that offends us to the point where we immediately get angry. These angry feelings flood your brain preventing you from thinking of anything else. They block your ability to think clearly and rationally.

We don't have to completely agree with the ideas of others, but we can listen to them realizing they've had their own unique experiences. Such openness to people means we quit trying to change them or their position, and approach each conversation with an open mind. This is how we can find common ground connections with even our strongest critics and people with whom we disagree.

We're not as divided as some people believe

While there are many people with angry and entrenched beliefs, others hold perceptions that are often similar on various issues. So what's the truth? Although the loudest, most divisive voices are often the only voices that are heard, they only represent a segment of the world's population. The largest number of people in every society hold a more moderate view of the world. They're also the least vocal. They want to get along with others regardless of their viewpoints. And they have hope for a more united future. Simply put, we agree more than we think we do. It may be time to start talking more about what unites not divides us.

The previous isn't meant to downplay the divisiveness in the world. But what's clear is that we have more to work with than we think we do when it comes to re-uniting the United States and the world. We're not totally divided as a human race, but we do need to work on our divisiveness now before it gets any worse.

"Where" do I start?

Each of us can start with our family, friends, work colleagues, and members of our community. I tell my brother who tells his friends at work who tell their respective families. The spread continues in this way on a timetable that can't really be determined. It can all start with a single one-on-one conversation and a change in emphasis on how we communicate.

Hope for future

In the United States, 93% of people say it's important to try to reduce divisiveness and believe that common ground can still be realized. This sentiment is echoed by 65% of the people throughout the world (Duffy & Gottfried, 2018).

In America at least, people remain optimistic about the country's future. Three-fourths of Americans believe that the differences between people are not so great that we can't come together (De Wit et al., 2019). Americans remain generally hopeful about the future of the country even as they are dissatisfied with the present state of the nation.

Changing lives

By seeking common ground connections in all areas of your life, you change not only your life but the lives of others in ways that you might not have thought possible. You become a model for how people can meaningfully communicate in a way that brings people together.

Bibliography

De Wit, L., Van der Linden, S., & Brick, C. (2019, July 2). What are the solutions to political polarization? Social psychology reveals what creates conflict among groups and how they come together. *Greater Good Magazine*.

Duffy, B., & Gottfried, G. (2018). *BBC global survey*. Ipsos MORI Research Institute.

INDEX

Printed in the United States
by Baker & Taylor Publisher Services